HIGHER ENGLISH: THE STUDENT GUIDE

CONTENTS

READ THIS FIRST

That was to get your attention.

You are probably like most people . . . you don't read the introduction until later. Please read this one now, because it's important for you to know how THE GUIDE works.

This introduction will tell you:

- why it's called HIGHER ENGLISH: THE STUDENT GUIDE
- what it will do for you
- what it cannot do for you
- why you and your teacher need THE GUIDE
- how and when to use it.

Why it's called HIGHER ENGLISH: THE STUDENT GUIDE

HIGHER ENGLISH: THE STUDENT GUIDE is aimed at a very particular reader. You are the particular reader for whom THE GUIDE is intended. You have seen the cover and the title, and they have attracted your attention, encouraging you to read this far.

That means that you are almost certainly a student either already in or going into fifth (or maybe sixth) year in school somewhere in Scotland. Or, you might be an adult or mature student in a college, or you may be working by yourself as an external candidate.

Whichever one of those categories you fit in to, the one thing that you have in common with all the others mentioned is that you are working hard at trying to pass your Higher English examinations at the end of this school year.

Passing the exam is very important to you.

You may need to get your Higher English because you hope to go on to higher education in a college or university. Without Higher English, your choice is very limited. It may be that, in the kind of job you are hoping for, employers demand a pass in English. It may be even simpler than that. You may have come to realise that an understanding of the language and literature of your country is something you should master if you are to take advantage of all the opportunities for a full life, not only now, but also later on.

What THE GUIDE will do for you

You have certainly come to the right place, and picked up the right book, for you will need help in your efforts. THE GUIDE is purpose-built to help you with the course in Higher English – at Higher or Intermediate level. At the time of writing, it's the only one. It is intended for you, the student. But maybe your teacher will have a look at it too. It's not a coursebook. It is a guide, with accurate and reliable information about the course and with a lot of valuable advice based on long experience, not only of teaching, but of marking, designing and setting examinations. As well as the information and the advice, there is guidance about what to do, and how to do it.

> THE GUIDE is designed to help you to understand very clearly what you should be doing in Higher English to make the best of your personal abilities.
>
> It will *not* be a substitute for your teacher or lecturer or tutor. It will *not* transform you into a genius in English without you having to do anything. If you work with your teacher and class, then THE GUIDE will help you to do much better than you would have done without it.
>
> There could not be a better time than right now to have THE GUIDE in your hands!

What THE GUIDE cannot do for you

At a time that now seems to me several centuries ago (it was definitely in the twentieth century and not the twenty-first), I used to teach an evening class in Higher English. The students who came to it were divided pretty much into two separate groups. What separated them was their attitude to the task, and their immediate past experience or history. One group consisted of 'mature' students who had come to try to get Higher English. Usually they were people who had left school as early as they could, years ago, and had missed their chance to sit the exams. Now they were back, knew exactly what they needed and were highly motivated, determined to do the best they could to succeed.

The second group was made up of people who had failed the exam the year before. They had left school and were now working . . . or, more often, they were 'looking for a job'. They had realised that they were being held back by the lack of the qualification they needed if they wanted to move upward in their job, or to find a job, or wanted to go on to higher education.

The difference between the first group and the second was not great – except in attitude and approach to the course.

The second group seemed to believe in a scientific principle – called osmosis. If you've done any biology, you'll know that this has to do with how plants take in water. It is just drawn in while the plant just sits there, so to speak. No effort made at all. These students operated in much the same way.

The idea was that if you . . .

- came to the class
- sat at the back of the room
- took little part in the work or activities
- but were just **there**

. . . then you would absorb all the skills, knowledge, understanding, competence and abilities through your skin. Just like plants and water.

Unfortunately, the teaching–learning process doesn't work in quite the same way as osmosis. It's a two-way arrangement: your teacher teaches and you learn. Learning is a positive activity, not a passive process. You can be taught, but only if you take part and actively learn.

So, *you* are important in this teaching–learning package.

In a kirkyard in Edinburgh (allegedly), there's a famous epitaph* on a gravestone that is over 300 years old.

Andro Meekie,

Late Parish Dominie

Beneath thir stanes lye Meekie's banes:
A Sawtan, gin ye tak him
Appeynt him tutor to your weans
An clever deils he'll mak 'em

1696

For those of you not fluent in the older Scots tongue, it says:

Andrew Meekie,

Late Master of the Parish School

Beneath these stones lie Meekie's bones:
O Satan, if you take him
Appoint him tutor to your children
And clever children he'll make them

1696

Now, whoever wrote that epitaph hadn't got it quite right. Even the brilliant teacher, Andrew Meekie, couldn't have made the Devil's children clever if they didn't want to learn. Your teacher will agree with that today. On a gravestone, however, the rule is 'Nil nisi bonum de mortuis' (Say only good about the dead).

So, the first thing you learn from THE GUIDE is that you have to take an active part in your course if you want to succeed.

Why you (and your teacher) need THE GUIDE

THE GUIDE tells you what you have to do 'examination-wise' or more accurately 'assessment-wise'. THE GUIDE doesn't do the actual teaching and is not trying to replace your teacher. Often it will be helping your teacher, because it is providing you with detailed information on what the examiners expect and require from you.

The teaching–learning package I mentioned just before Meekie's epitaph consists of three parts. THE GUIDE is based on a Deal and there are three parties to this agreement, three parts of the package:

1 The important one – you

2 THE GUIDE itself

3 Your teacher.

If all three parts work together, then you will certainly end up more aware, more confident and a lot more able than you would otherwise be.

So, do you want to sign up to the Deal? **TICK HERE** to show you'll do your bit: ☐

How and when to use THE GUIDE

You can draft in more partners to your part of the Deal, if you like. A very helpful way of working is to convince a friend and classmate to buy a copy of the book (this is not just an advertisement) and then for the two of you to work together as 'study buddies'. As the old saying has it, 'Two heads are better than one'. In this way, the two of you will generate much more motivation and learning than you could do alone.

You should read THE GUIDE straight through at least once to begin with. After that you can return for clarification, since the first reading of material of this kind often seems puzzling until you have gained more information and knowledge.

You will acquire both of these during the course, and you should always seek your teacher's help throughout the course. Then, you can use THE GUIDE as you require at various times throughout the course, dipping in to specific sections covering separate components of the course as they come up in class.

Language

I have tried to write THE GUIDE in a straightforward style of language that sets out to be clear and simple, but without patronising you. This is an important feature of the book, because it aims to bring home to you the central messages of the rulebook for the Higher English course and examinations – the *Arrangements for English and Communication* – which is written in jargon* . . . and is written for teachers.

Jargon is not necessarily a pejorative* term (we do aim to improve your knowledge here and there, and the use of words is one of the areas that can be improved). Words that are marked with an asterisk, like epitaph, jargon and pejorative in this Introduction, are explained in the glossary at the end of the book.

Health warning!

At the time of writing, it is impossible to end this introduction without saying something about the situation surrounding what is still being called Higher Still. In 2000, public faith in the assessment agency, the Scottish Qualifications Authority (SQA), was badly dented by well-publicised problems in producing results for students. What may or may not have contributed to the problems was the very great degree of internal assessment data that is required by SQA to determine the overall awards made to students. Collection of this data should have very little impact on what you do when learning on the course, taking the internal assessments and sitting the external examinations. These activities go on independently of the certification process and you should try to pay very little attention to any possible problems in that area – because such problems simply should not affect your learning or your teacher's delivery of the course.

Partly as a result of the problems described, and partly because Higher Still English has not bedded down in anything like the way other subjects have, it is more than possible that the Arrangements described in detail in THE GUIDE will be changed over time. A further consultation of the teaching profession is currently taking place and may lead to changes. These changes, if they take place, will be well advertised and your teacher will know about them. The good news is that possible changes are likely to reduce the demand on time and perhaps assessment, but it is unlikely that you would be expected to do more than is described here in THE GUIDE.

This means that you should always check with your teacher that the current edition of THE GUIDE matches the latest Arrangements. You can also check for yourself on the SQA website – www.sqa.org.uk

HIGHER (STILL) ENGLISH:

HOW IT ALL WORKS

Out with the old, in with the new

I'm sure you don't think that you're all that fortunate to be doing Higher English – it's probably not what comes to mind when someone asks what you like doing. You just know that you **have** to do it. You are, however, certainly lucky to be doing it at this particular time.

Unlike your teachers, by starting your Higher course **now:**

- **you** won't have to make a change from a system that you have been using for years.

- **you** won't have to 'unlearn' what has become very familiar to you.

- **you** won't be nagged by doubts that this isn't as good a system as the one you were used to.

- **you** are just entering a new course. It is just a different new thing that you have to get used to, and carry on.

Bear in mind, this isn't the experience that your teacher is having. Perhaps for a good few years from the time you are reading this, your teachers might still be finding the Higher system (or, to give it its formal title, the National Qualifications, NQ) awkward and difficult to operate. It certainly is very different from what they have been used to.

The old Higher English course

The problem for teachers is that they have to **unlearn** the previous system. You don't have that problem, obviously, as I've said. That gives you quite an advantage here. It means, for one thing, that you don't have to read through pages about what went before, and then follow all the changes. So, we can get straight on to a clear explanation of how the Higher English system works. It may seem odd, but you are going to be able to adapt to the new system more easily than your teachers will, at first. For you, it's no more difficult than it would have been if nothing had changed: both the old system and this new system would have been new to you.

Having just said that we are not going through the old Higher system, it might seem somewhat odd to mention it again right away, but I'm going to . . . so that the explanation of the new system will be even clearer.

It is very likely that you have just completed a course and exams in English at Standard Grade. Most students arrive at the Higher English course that way, and are in fifth (S5) year at a school. If that description doesn't fit you, just bear with us for a moment or two, till we get past the next few paragraphs or so.

Higher English for you is rather like Standard Grade in some ways, but it certainly isn't very much like the old Higher which it is replacing.

We can pass over the explanation of the old system quickly. All you need to know about it is that it operated at one level – Higher Grade – and that there was a single course leading to an external examination. You would send in a folio of coursework for external assessment by SQA. At the end of the course, you would sit an examination on a (nice sunny!) day in May. Your award and certificate was decided mainly by what you did in the folio and in the examination on that day.

That was Higher Grade, as it was: teaching done by the schools; assessment (either of submitted coursework or written examination papers) done by the external agency (now SQA). There was no *internal* assessment.

The new Higher English course
A comparison with Standard Grade

If, like most readers of this guide, you've just arrived in S5 this year, then you won't really have to be reminded too much of things from Standard Grade like:

- working for your folio
- going through the assessment of talking activities.

> These two features of Standard Grade are the two aspects that make it quite like parts of the new Higher that you are going to take this year.

The folio at Standard Grade was the clearest marker that coursework played an important part in the scheme. The work in reading and writing was coursework. (Remember the two writing pieces and the three reading essays that you had to work on and redraft – and sometimes re-re-redraft – and then had to take care of till it was time to send in your folio?)

The folio was completed in class during the course, and then sent in to SQA to be marked externally. The writing and reading pieces together made up one-third of the value of the whole award.

The talking element was carried out in the class during the course, but it was assessed by your teacher, that is, internally. Talking was also worth one-third of the whole award.

Finally, you sat the examinations in May, one in reading and the other in writing. The SQA markers marked these papers, so the assessment of the exam was completely external. These two exams together made up the remaining one-third of the value of the whole award.

Old Higher Grade and Standard Grade compared

So, when both (old) Higher Grade and Standard Grade are set out in a grid (Table 1.1) for comparison, you can see clearly how they differ.

TABLE 1.1 ASSESSMENT ARRANGEMENTS FOR STANDARD GRADE AND (OLD) HIGHER GRADE

	Internal assessment	Coursework	External/ exam assessment
Standard Grade	Yes	Yes	Yes
Higher Grade (old)	No	Yes	Yes

The two Grades, Standard and the old Higher, were quite different in their course content as well as in their assessment systems. Look at these grids (Tables 1.2 and 1.3) to see what they each contained. They also show how the various components or elements contributed to the award.

TABLE 1.2 COURSE CONTENT FOR STANDARD GRADE

Talking	Examination	Folio
Internal assessment	External assessment	Internally generated/ Externally assessed
• Individual talk	• Writing 16.66%	• Writing (2) 16.66%
• Discussion 33.33%	• Reading 16.66%	• Reading (3) 16.66%

TABLE 1.3 COURSE CONTENT FOR (OLD) HIGHER GRADE

Paper 1	Paper 2	Folio
External assessment	External assessment	Internally generated/ externally assessed
Interpretation 20%	Practical criticism *or*	Review of Personal Reading (20%)
Report 18%	Close reading texts 13% Critical Essay 15%	Imaginative discursive writing 13%

Summary

At Standard Grade there was:

1   internal assessment of coursework (talking)

2   external assessment of exam work (reading and writing)

3   external assessment of coursework (folio reading/writing).

At (old) Higher Grade there was:

1   external assessment of coursework (folio)

2   external assessment of exam work (reading and writing).

How does Higher English now compare?

Let's get on to the Higher as you are going to experience it. I want to explain the system of levels.

Levels

'Getting your Highers' now means different things to different people. When the old Higher Grade examination was first introduced in 1880 or so, it was intended that it would be used as the qualification to certify the highest level of achievement for school leavers going on to higher education or into one of the so-called learned professions (then, medicine, law, the Church, teaching, etc.). So, it was a qualification aimed at a very small percentage of the population.

Life has changed very much, and a great many more people than formerly now need to have qualifications so that they can pursue careers and ways of life that are widely varying. As a result, it has been necessary to provide a range of qualifications. This range includes various **levels**, **subjects** and **types** of qualification.

What we have been calling Higher English is now just one level of a more complicated system. It fits into a hierarchy* of levels of a course offered in Higher Still/National Qualifications. So, over the span of the two final years of schooling (S5 and S6), you could theoretically be attempting to gain an award (a certificate) from a range that comprises* the following levels:

- Advanced Higher
- Higher
- Intermediate 2
- Intermediate 1
- Access.

I say 'theoretically' because, in real life, most students will attempt only one of these levels.

A minority (roughly 2000 out of roughly 35000) of students in S6 will take Advanced Higher after having completed Higher in S5. The number in S5/S6 who will take Intermediate 2 or 1 is not yet clear. These students would not attempt Higher in S5 but might go on to attempt it in S6. In S5 most students will take Higher or Intermediate 2 or 1 or Access.

In S6, of those who took Intermediate 2, some will attempt Higher: and some who took Intermediate 1 will attempt Intermediate 2. The number of such students will be very small.

> In THE GUIDE, we are dealing only with Higher, and to some extent, Intermediate 2.

Academic and Vocational

National Qualifications (you might find it being called 'Higher Still' for some time yet, for that's what it was called in the development stage) contains both kinds of qualifications – academic and vocational – though that distinction is being removed. English was one of the 'academic' qualifications. The new system also contains qualifications at different levels of achievement and a great many options. How the options affect you is explained in this chapter, in the next chapter, and also in the later individual chapters on the units. This brings us to the next feature of the National Qualifications: the unit system.

The unit system

Units are like Lego; building bricks for the course. The basic brick is a 40-hour teaching and assessment package. Each one deals with a separate element or component of the subject. This applies to all subjects, not only to English.

The Higher English course is made up of such units, some compulsory, some optional. Within each of the units, whether it is an optional one or a compulsory one, there are choices. So the units you choose might not be the same as the ones your friends choose – and even if you do choose the same units as each other, the actual content of the unit and what is assessed can differ. In the classroom, except when it comes to the assessment times, you'll hardly notice the unit structure as a feature of the course. Though most English teaching will be holistic*, you do have to understand how the units feature in the system because you need a certain group of unit qualifications to help make up your final award.

The units in English

In the Higher English course, you will take the following compulsory units:

Unit 1	Language Studies Unit	40 hours
Unit 2	Literary Studies Unit	40 hours
Unit 3	Oral communication Unit	20 hours
Unit 4	Specialist study Unit	20 hours

There will also be another 40 hours not directly taken up with any one unit. So the course nominally* takes up 160 hours (40 + 40 + 20 + 20 + 40): most students spend more time than that on it, of course. They work out of school time as well as in school time.

Students taking Higher English have always had to spend much more time on their studies than was ever available in the classroom alone. This is an idea that it would be good to get hold of early on in your course. Quite a lot is said about it further on in the sections dealing with motivation and working practices (Chapter 3).

You already know that there will be choices within both the 'full' (40-hour) units and wider options in the 'half' (20-hour) units. The list above is only an outline. A fuller specification follows on pages 12–13 and the details on choices and options are set out in the individual unit chapters further on in THE GUIDE, with advice on *how* to choose, though less on *what* to choose.

Compulsory course content

This section is very short. There isn't any choice here if you are working towards a course award. If you are (very improbably) simply working for unit awards, internally assessed, then the requirements are slightly different. You wouldn't be sitting the external examinations, and you wouldn't be expecting to get 'your Highers'.

The compulsory, non-negotiable requirements for a NQ award of Intermediate 2 English or Higher English are:

1 compulsory units

2 compulsory folio

3 compulsory examination.

It is important to note that while you have to complete the compulsory units, you have some choice about the actual detailed content of some of the units you attempt. These choices you can negotiate with your teacher.

Units

The previous page (look back at it now) shows a quick summary list of the units.

This is just a quick outline of the first compulsory component of this course – the units. Each unit is dealt with in detail further on in THE GUIDE (Chapters 4–8).

Unit 1 (Language Studies) and Unit 2 (Literary Studies)

Unit 1 (Language Studies) and Unit 2 (Literary Studies) both have limited content options within them, so we'll come back to those in Chapters 5 and 6, dealing with each of them in detail.

As well as those two units, you must also complete two more units in which your options are much greater in the form you choose to offer.

Unit 3 (Oral communication)

Unit 3 (Oral communication) is all on oral skills, but here you have a choice of three different types:

- Unit 3A – Individual presentation

or

- Unit 3B – Group discussion

or

- Unit 3C – Critical listening.

You 'choose' only one from 3A, 3B and 3C.

Unit 4 (Specialist Study)

Unit 4, (Specialist study) also offers you a choice of three different types. You can choose to produce a written piece on either language or literature or you can choose to deliver a spoken presentation on some aspect of oral communication. Put simply, you can choose either to write about writing and reading, or to talk about talking and listening! This is dealt with in detail in Chapter 7. The specialist study becomes part of your folio, which goes to SQA for external assessment.

If you read the above and look at the course specification below at the same time, both the specification itself and these words will be clearer than either separately.

Course specification

Unit 1	Language Studies	(40 hours)
Unit 2	Literary Studies	(40 hours)
Unit 3A	Individual presentation	(20 hours)

or

| Unit 3B | Group discussion | (20 hours) |

or

| Unit 3C | Critical listening | (20 hours) |
| Unit 4A | Specialist study – language | (20 hours) |

or

| Unit 4B | Specialist study – literature | (20 hours) |

or

| Unit 4C | Specialist study – oral communication | (20 hours) |

The folio

Second of the three compulsory parts of the course is the folio.

The idea of a folio is familiar to you already if you have done English at Standard Grade. One important point to grasp about it, however, is how misunderstood it has been in many schools. The folio is meant to contain pieces of work that you have completed as part of your course. You may remember 'working for your folio', as if it was something completely separate from the real activities of the Standard Grade course. It is not meant to be a collection of separate, specially-produced items for the purpose of the folio.

For the Higher course, there won't be that difficulty, anyway. Everything in the folio will have been part of a unit, so the folio is a kind of sampling. In other words your folio will be completed by you as part of your coursework in the four units, and your teacher/school/college will send everything in it to SQA at Dalkeith. There, it will be externally assessed.

Your folio is a compulsory part of the course if you are to gain a **course award** rather than just **unit credits**. It has three parts, or items, and each part is compulsory. Each part, however, has three options within it.

The three compulsory folio items are:

- Item 1 – Writing
- Item 2 – Oral /aural communication
- Item 3 – Specialist study

These items are produced by you as unit requirements – a clear demonstration that they are being completed as part of the course, and are not really separate additional pieces of work that you have to do. You do them as part of your work in different units; your teacher assesses them as part of the unit credit; and then they are sent in to SQA for final external assessment.

Let's look at each of these items individually for a moment. The full details of each are described in Chapters 5, 7 and 8.

Item 1 – Writing

You do **one** piece of writing, choosing **one** of these forms:

1   expressive writing

2   creative writing

3   a report.

As you have by now probably come to expect, there are choices for you to make within each of these forms of writing, but we'll deal with those in the section of THE GUIDE dealing with the folio (Chapter 9), as well as in the section on Unit 1 (Chapter 5).

Item 2 – Oral/aural communication

The oral/aural item in your folio will simply be a mark for oral work you've already done in the course, and this will be sent in to SQA by your teacher. The mark will be for one of the following:

1   individual presentation

2   group discussion

3   critical listening.

The form that your oral/aural work takes depends on which one of these you (or perhaps your school) have/has chosen to do in Unit 3.

There is much more about the oral part of the course later on in THE GUIDE in the section dealing with the units (Chapter 7).

Item 3 – Specialist study

The specialist study (already mentioned) is the major contribution to the folio. It will be taken from your work in Unit 4 and what it consists of will depend on your choice. For most students it will be a longish essay on some topic in literature (based on Unit 1) or some aspect of language (based on Unit 2) that you will have chosen for yourself, but with your teacher's advice and guidance. I suspect that you are much more likely to chose the literature option than the language one, and even less likely to choose to base your specialist study on Unit 3 (the oral/aural unit options), but we'll discuss that later in Chapter 8.

> You will write the specialist study under controlled conditions as it is very important to make sure that it really is all your own work.

If you choose to do your specialist study on some topic in oral communication (based on Unit 3), then your folio item will not be written. It has to be done as a video presentation.

1　Don't be misled into thinking that a video presentation is an easy option compared to a written study. The same standards apply.

2　There is a rule limiting your choices: if you choose to do individual presentation in your oral communication unit (Unit 3), then your specialist study (Unit 4) mustn't be about individual presentation. Obviously that would be covering the same ground twice and using very similar skills.

The examinations

The final part of the package that you have to complete for the course award – Higher or Intermediate 2 English – is the examination at the end of the course. This section is a brief outline. The full details of the examination are provided in Chapter 10.

The exam is set by the Scottish Qualifications Authority, as your Standard Grade exams were. Your work is externally assessed by SQA examiners. In plain language, that simply means that your teachers do not mark your papers, as they did for the unit assessment.

Some time later, your results come to you in that familiar brown envelope with your own handwriting on it – the envelope everybody dreads.

The dreaded brown envelope

The exam takes three hours altogether and consists of two separate papers: an hour and a half for each.

Paper I – Interpretation (now officially called close reading)

There are no options here. You will have two unseen passages of prose and questions about **each** of them separately, as well as questions about **both** of them together.

The questions will test your close reading skills, mainly the skills that you will have been dealing with in Unit 1 of the course. Broadly, these are to do with language.

Paper II – Analysis and appreciation

This paper is divided into two parts. In the first part – called textual analysis – you will be dealing with one unseen piece of literature. It could be poetry or prose or drama, but the examiners make that choice. You don't have any choice here. Questions on it will deal with the literary values of the writing, as well as the meaning. You will be using the skills you have developed in studying works of literature as part of Unit 2 in the course.

The second part of the paper – called critical essay – is also about literature. Here you will have a choice. You will write an essay about any one of the pieces of literature you have studied: poetry or prose or drama or a mass media text.

Weighting of the different forms of assessment

Before we move to the next chapter, there is something else to think about. Higher English, the award you are working for, is based on the two different assessment components, the folio and the examination:

- The folio is worth 40% of the marks available.

- The exam is worth 60%.

Assessment

As you saw in the section about Standard Grade, not all parts of the course can be covered by examinations, so other forms of assessment had to be devised.

- Some parts of the English course are covered by **internal assessment**.

- Some have **external assessment** by examinations.

- Some parts are assessed by a cross between the two **(internally generated/externally assessed)**.

As part of the structure of Scottish qualifications, the Scottish **Qualifications** Authority (SQA) was set up to be responsible for all qualifications, both academic and vocational. National Qualifications co-ordinates these and uses both internal and external assessment. Internal assessment is used for the units in schools. External assessment is used in the examinations and for the folio.

The National Qualifications also includes that hybrid form of assessment already mentioned, internally produced/externally assessed. Indeed, assessment will become a familiar matter to you during your course. It will also be an important part of what you experience during your time in the Higher class.

One feature of the unit system is that there will be end-of-unit assessment. Your teacher will set the tasks or tests, and will also assess your work. Obviously, therefore, it's internal assessment. Mostly, the tests will be provided to the school by the SQA. These tests are commonly called NABS (National Assessment Banks).

Students who have already taken the course in 1999–2000 – and there were very few of them – have reported that the main feature that they found troublesome was the emphasis on assessment. It may be that the system, as it evolves, will reduce the frequency and form of internal assessment requirements. Changes are taking place at the time this is being written, perhaps also at the time that you are reading this, as already noted in the introduction. If you've skipped it, now is the time to stop, go back and read it.

Because assessment (not exams) is a prominent feature of the National Qualifications arrangements, this chapter will be using the assessment structure quite a lot to explain the scheme to you. This section of the guide will feel a bit like assessment, assessment, and more assessment. Later in the guide the emphasis will return to the equally important matters of teaching and learning in the course.

In English, it's not likely that any school will deal with the units completely separately from each other, either in the teaching or in the assessing. It would be difficult and also very artificial to try to take the units one by one, in order. As you can probably figure out for yourself, the structure of English teaching and learning is not at all like the systems that suit some other subjects. Some subjects have a great deal of what we would call content. To exaggerate and caricature subjects like this, we could say that they consist of learning a lot of factual information – dates, formulae, vocabulary, rules, etc.

To caricature English in the same way, we could say that it consists of learning the same things more intensively, revisiting ideas and concepts* that have already been treated at earlier stages. Neither of these caricatures is, of course, completely true. Using exaggeration (or hyperbole*) is a literary device, and often its purpose is to help to make a point more clearly. Everyone sees the exaggeration, realising that it isn't completely accurate, of course, but it helps to polarise* the argument, making clear the distinction that's being attempted.

I hope that you have used the glossary to find the meanings of the asterisked words I'm deliberately using here. It is a good idea to always be trying to increase your vocabulary. How you do that is by looking up words you come across in your reading, or to ask about them quite openly . . . and then, importantly, use them in your speaking and writing.

So, you shouldn't expect in English (though you just might in some other subjects) to study one unit at a time and then, when it's completed, have a unit assessment for that unit only . . . all before you go on to the next unit. You'll be dealing with parts of each and all of the units at the same time, and progressing through them all simultaneously. For this reason, you can expect to have internal assessments (perhaps wee tests) at various stages of the course. This is why you will be quite firmly aware of the assessment side of Higher English, as well as of the teaching and learning side of things.

Now some important information about unit assessment

Before you can gain a Higher in English, you have to pass each of the units of the course.

Read that sentence again very carefully.

It means that you will not normally be awarded a Higher if you don't have a pass in the units. You can think of the unit assessments as a kind of passport to the Higher English, if you like.

There are three other things to be said about this, however, and they are also very important:

1   You can *sit the exam* without having achieved everything required in the unit assessment.

2   You can *pass the exam* and still not get your Higher award.

3   You can *gain the award* in very special and unusual circumstances by sitting and passing the exam even if you have not completed the unit assessment.

These three statements deal with exceptions, and you would be best to think that passing all the unit assessments first and then sitting the exam is the normal way to deal with getting your Higher English. The puzzle is solved when you see that sitting the exam, passing the exam, and gaining the certificate are three completely different things.

These points are explained in detail in Chapters 4–8. To explain it now would just be confusing for you: we'll leave it until you know more about the system.

There is one other very important piece of information that you should understand right now about internal unit assessment. It is re-assessment.

Re-assessment

Each unit has certain requirements that you must fulfil in order to pass the unit when your teacher assesses your work. These are called **outcomes**, and the number of outcomes you must achieve varies from unit to unit. The outcomes have attached to them what are called **performance criteria**. These are the markers used in the assessment to decide whether you are successful or not – or whether the work is of an acceptable standard. Assessments will take different forms: there might be tests with questions, there might be a single piece of writing to complete, and so on.

Many of these assessment 'instruments', as they are called, will have been produced by SQA as part of a National Assessment Bank. They come with marking instructions and 'answers', so that your teacher will be using the same materials and marking systems as other schools. They won't be just operating an assessment system that they have made up themselves. You can be fairly confident that the internal assessments will be correctly made, and will be operating to a standard that is as consistent as it can be across the country.

Now, you can either pass or fail in any of these assessments. If you pass, that's fine. It's recorded, and you go on to achieve similar success in the other outcomes of the unit.

If you fail, however, it's not the end of the world. You can have one more attempt (or, exceptionally, two more attempts) to pass. But you can't have repeated attempts at the *same* test. If you were to fail repeatedly, it would probably mean that you were attempting the wrong level of the course in English and that you should really be trying a lower one.

I am sure you are starting to see why assessment is going to be an important and prominent activity in the course.

Examinations

I've use the word 'assessment' up till now because 'exams' is a word that doesn't cover the assessment system fully, as at one time it did. It's best now to think of the exams as a *part* of the assessment system – some people would say the most important part. The whole assessment system includes internal assessments of the units, external assessment of coursework and at the end of the course, an externally assessed examination consisting of two papers of three hours in total. But there's quite a lot to be done and not a lot of time in which to do it.

The Scottish Qualifications Authority has an unique system of appeals to offset the effect of having a bad hair day at the exams, something that is familiar to many people. It sounds odd, but you can fail the exam on the day, and still pass . . . if you have been doing work in class that merits a pass. There's more on this much later on (Chapter 10), when we look at what to do about an appeal*.

The full details of the exam are set out later on in THE GUIDE (Chapter 10). The standard required for a pass in the exam is exactly the same as in the old Higher. The value of the award you are trying to achieve is the same as it has been from the time Higher English was introduced in the 1880s. That means that your Higher should be equivalent to mine!

The next chapter of THE GUIDE deals with the system of levels introduced by Higher Still.

CHAPTER TWO

THE LEVELS AND YOU

Making choices

Chapter 1 gave a broad outline of how the Higher system is designed. Some areas are compulsory and in other parts you have a choice of different options. We should be realistic about these choices, however. You will find that some selections have already been made for you by your teacher.

The *Arrangements for Higher English* go to great lengths about the importance of choices for the student. This section is to help you understand *where* you have a choice and *what* you can choose from. You will need to understand this when you negotiate with your teacher. Making the right choices will mean that you get the best out of the course, using the strengths that you already have and learning the skills that you will need.

Can you choose a level?

It may be that you have already been assigned to a particular level of the course. School resources and English department policy often mean that the options in what is offered have to be limited. As well as that, you have to accept that you cannot always do exactly what *you* want to do. Sometimes you can negotiate to get your preference, but at other times it won't be possible.

Your teacher will be trying always to match your abilities and your interests with what is on offer and with what is demanded by the assessment standards. Your teacher will try to assign you to a level of the course that you can cope with reasonably, or which presents you with an achievable challenge. There is obviously no point in having you attempt a level which is clearly beyond your capacity: nor is it helpful to decide your 'options' for you if you have no interest or ability in the ones that are chosen. No sensible teacher will do that – it leads only to grief all round. There is a certain amount of flexibility built into the National Qualifications system that will help you and your teacher to settle the level at which you should be working.

There are difficult decisions sometimes. If you are a brilliant genius or if you are at the opposite end of the spectrum*, then the decisions about what level you'll be attempting are pretty straightforward. Unfortunately, most people are to be found in the middle of that spectrum of ability. The trick is to make sure that you are neither struggling to keep up with the course, nor finding the level chosen so easy that you feel that you're wasting your time. Between you, your teacher and you should be able to negotiate a set of choices in the course and the assessment requirements that allow you to:

- take your teacher's advice
- indulge your interests
- build on your strengths
- achieve success rather than failure
- work towards clear targets for your learning
- develop understanding
- make progress.

Course entry level

To some extent you should be able to negotiate with your teacher about the level of the course you are taking. Mostly, however, the decision is inevitable, since the entry level for each course is based on what you have already achieved. The entry levels are only recommended though, and that allows for some flexibility in negotiating.

Have a look at Table 2.1. It will help you make some *preliminary* decisions about what you should be doing in your Higher year.

As you saw at the very beginning of this book, we have assumed that you are reading this because you're starting your Higher year, and you've already completed Standard Grade with an award at Credit or General. If your award at Standard Grade was at Foundation Level you would attempt Intermediate 1 or Access Level, however those are outside the scope of THE GUIDE.

THE GUIDE is intended to help you if you are attempting the course at Higher or Intermediate 2.

TABLE 2.1 ENTRY LEVELS FOR DIFFERENT HIGHER ENGLISH COURSES

Your existing award (your entry level)		NQ equivalent		Your course level
Standard Grade General	=	Intermediate 1	→	Intermediate 2
Standard Grade Credit	=	Intermediate 2	→	Higher

Remember that you should be moving **upwards** from whatever you have already achieved at Standard Grade.

So, have a quick look at the left-hand column, check what you have already got, and read across to the middle column. The middle column shows you what equivalent level you have already achieved at National Qualifications. Now, move across to the third column. This tells you the level of course you ought to be attempting now.

In the same way, if you are in S6 and took Intermediate 1 or 2 in S5, you can start in column two and find your level for this year's course in column three. Only a small minority of students will be in this position.

It's important for you to see why you should be attempting a course at a particular level. This helps to make sure that you have realistic choices and sensible expectations. You will see from Table 2.1 that we can really look only at Intermediate 2 and Higher as possible course level choices for you.

If your award at Standard Grade was Foundation Level, you could certainly aim for Intermediate 1 as your course level and use this book as your guide, but Intermediate 1 won't be mentioned much by name. Since the general *shape* of the course is the same at Intermediate 1 as at Intermediate 2 and Higher, everything said about them applies to Intermediate 1. Only the standard of performance the examiners expect from you in the coursework and examinations is different . . . and sometimes the actual pieces of work differ in number or type as well. So, if you are attempting Intermediate 1, though THE GUIDE can help you to understand the system and what you have to do, read it with care — and always check with your teacher.

MAKING THE MOST OF YOUR ABILITIES

So far, so good

If you have read this far, you will now have formed a good idea of how the Higher English system works, with the course and the units that make it up. You will have realised the importance of the parallel assessment system – the internal and the external aspects.

Now it's time to deal with how to tackle these *challenges*.

Motivation

Note that I have just referred to what you have to do as *challenges*, not as difficulties or obstacles. Always think positively about your Higher English course. It will help you to achieve your best if you can see Higher English in this light. It will hold you back if you view the course in a negative way.

Higher English is by no means unattainable. In the Introduction I suggested that you think of the work toward your Higher English as a kind of contract or deal that you make. There are three partners in the deal:

1 you

2 THE GUIDE

3 your teacher.

The ingredients that you have to contribute are:

- your ability
- your work
- your willingness.

A single word that encompasses all three of these is **motivation**.

You have to want to pass Higher English, and you have to be willing to do what it takes to get it. It won't just happen, no matter how much you wish for it, without action.

THE GUIDE will support you by giving you:

- information
- advice
- support and encouragement
- some practice.

Your teacher will contribute exactly these same things, but with the added advantage of being right *there* to interact with you in the classroom. Keep in mind that teaching is an interactive arrangement: it cannot take place unless there is also learning going on. That's what you contribute to the deal, remember?

Overall, without the contribution of all three partners, the plan won't work. Remember that the intention of the plan is to make sure that you are given the best chance possible of passing your Higher English.

Demonstrating all the skills required

Even though you have choices in Higher English, you cannot get away with doing only certain things, showing that you have certain skills, but failing completely to demonstrate any ability in some others. As has been said earlier, the learning and assessment of that learning in Higher English is *holistic* – you gain a pass overall in the examinations by aggregating (simply adding together) marks from the various parts. But you do not have to succeed in each and every one of the skills and components in a 'ticky-box' kind of arrangement.

Performance criteria and outcomes

In the **unit assessments** there is a range of demands, and you will be required to demonstrate an *acceptable* level of competence in each of the outcomes and performance criteria to gain overall success. But you do not have to be equally proficient in each and every skill: the level of your abilities across the range of requirements is likely to be variable. But you always have to reach the *minimum level* in each outcome before your teacher will decide that you have achieved a pass in that unit. So don't expect to pass in a unit until you have achieved the standard set down for each outcome: you can't pass Higher English by doing well in some areas and not well in others, expecting the successes to compensate for the failures.

In the external examination (since this tests your abilities in a sample of all the skills and abilities you have already demonstrated in the unit assessments), you certainly don't have to succeed in every part of the examination in order to pass. You can see sense in this. Can you imagine an examination where you had to pass in each and every question before you could pass the whole examination?

Avoiding complacency

There's something else you should think about that is invaluable* on the road to success. You must avoid complacency*.

One of the features of the NQ system is that the outcomes and the performance criteria are published for all to see. Nothing wrong with that, you'll agree. The danger lies in how they are written.

The outcomes simply state what a candidate (that is **you**) has to be able to do in order to 'achieve the outcome'. The performance criteria provide a little more detail by describing the basic performance requirement. In other words, they say what is the *least* you have to do to succeed. The danger is that many people read what is the least they have to do and aim for that as their target.

Aiming for the lowest level of acceptability is not what you could call positive thinking. It won't *motivate* you. If you intend to make a real success of your course, start thinking of it as the way to education and learning . . . not as hurdle-jumping in order to get it done and get it over with. If you think positively, your expectations are raised and you are far more likely to do better in the challenges that you tackle.

Combating teacher expectation

There is a phenomenon* called 'teacher expectation'. Put simply, students perform as well as, or as badly as, their teacher expects them to, if the expectation is made known to the students. If the expectation is high, this is fine. If expectation is low, this is not at all fine.

Two things that defeat low teacher expectation are: positive thinking and confidence in your own ability. So these are things that you should bring with you to the course, right from the beginning. Hard work, determination, an enquiring mind, motivation and your own natural ability are useful too. Positive encouragement (rather than low expectation) from your teacher is indispensable. Try to earn it. Be interested, enthusiastic and enquiring.

Don't think 'How little can I get away with? What is the least I have to do to pass?'. If you already think like that, and if you are not prepared to change from that thinking, you won't get very far.

Peer pressure

We all know that since you are a teenager, you're supposed to be completely incapable of making any real decisions for yourself; that you are always going to be influenced by that mysterious thing called 'peer-group pressure'! It's a compulsion to tend to do what your pals do, especially if they think it's cool. Depending on the particular fashion of the time, being brainy or swotty at school can be regarded, especially among boys, as definitely uncool.

You really have to forget that kind of thinking. You have to think: what is important right now, and in the future what is going to matter to *me*? Positive thinking and confidence in yourself will help you to see that working for what you want and need is something your peer group would all do too, if only they had the real sense and courage to make up their own minds, and stick to it.

CHAPTER FOUR

THE LANGUAGE STUDIES UNIT:

CLOSE READING

Interpretation and writing

The Language Studies Unit has two parts, interpretation (or close reading) and writing. These reflect the two outcomes of the unit.

Opportunities for making choices

There are many choices in this unit. After these choices have been described and the rules explained, there will be advice about how to choose.

The reasons for recommending certain choices and not others are as follows.

- Your school or college may not offer all the options available.

- Some options are regarded as less likely to lead you to success.

- Some are notoriously tedious in teaching and learning.

- Some consume disproportionately too much of the course time and, consequently, leave less time available for teaching, learning and assessment of other skills.

> Whatever advice on choices you read here in THE GUIDE, you are perfectly free to disregard. Take other advice locally . . . that will inevitably mean from your teacher.

Being aware of how we use language

This unit is all about language, and language operates in several different ways. You will very seldom use language in one particular mode* isolated from the others. Reading and writing are activities that you might say are each 'just one thing', but, if you think about it, you'll find that you do both together. I'm writing at the moment, but I'm also reading what I am writing and even talking (sometimes to myself).

So, when we write, we also read, we talk, and we listen. That is exactly how your course and the units it contains will be happening. Although this unit is about close reading and writing, that certainly does not mean that you will abandon all the other modes of language.

What the *Arrangements* say

To start with, we are going to look at material relating to Outcome 1 (close reading). Some of what you will find in this section is taken directly from the *Arrangements*. We are going to see what the *Arrangements* say about:

- the outcome itself
- the activities of the unit
- the texts used in the unit
- the performance criteria
- the evidence requirements.

Anything taken from the *Arrangements* will be followed by whatever translation is needed for you, including explanation, commentary, advice and illustration of the various points.

For the other outcome, writing, and for all the other units, I'll try to avoid as far as possible the direct wording of the *Arrangements*, and go straight into plain-language 'translations' of the requirements. The exact wording of the *Arrangements* seen once will be enough to let you see what it looks like, and you'll probably agree that you don't want to have it regurgitated* for each of the units.

Remember that this Language Studies Unit is just one part of the course; that you will spend about 40 hours on this unit; but that you will not be carrying out the Language Studies Unit activities in isolation from the activities for the other units of the course.

We can artificially isolate the language activities by listing them as outcomes in the same way that the *Arrangements* document does. These activities allow you to hone the skills required for interpretation. Many of these skills will be used in other parts of the course as well, of course.

Outcomes

In the Language Studies Unit, you have to fulfil these two outcomes:

> *Outcome 1 Understand, analyse and evaluate non-fiction print text which conveys complex information.*
>
> *Outcome 2 Compose a piece of writing in a particular genre.*

In other words, Outcome 1 is where you do **interpretation** (or **close reading**) and Outcome 2 is **writing**.

As I mentioned, we're leaving the writing outcome till later and dealing first with the interpretation (Outcome 1).

You will find the terms 'interpretation' and 'close reading' used interchangeably. From now on I'm going to refer to it as **close reading** because this is what it is called on the exam paper.

Activities

Activities are how you cover the outcomes. It has already been pointed out that, except perhaps at the end of unit assessment, you won't be carrying out separate activities for each outcome. The reason for this is easy to understand. The activities often have two sides to them; one side is connected more with close reading (what you take in). The other side has more to do with writing/expressing (what you give out). To bring out this distinction and at the same time to show the linkage between them, the close reading activities are set in bold type below. The other bits reflect the writing outcome of the unit.

analysing and using **different reading skills/purposes**

analysing and using **different writing skills/purposes**

deploying different research techniques

keeping records

identifying sources

creating banks of information

evaluating sources/texts

synthesising information and ideas

identifying and manipulating **points of view**

analysing and using **persuasive techniques**

creating writing workshops

examining model texts and structures

analysing and using **literary and linguistic devices and techniques**

constructing and manipulating different forms

analysing and using **different questioning techniques**

individual and collaborative talk

It may come as a bit of a surprise that talk is included here, but when we come to Chapter 7 of THE GUIDE, dealing with oral/aural skills, you'll recognise why it's here as a part of the activities concerning close reading.

So, according to the *Arrangements*, this is what you'll be doing. Now for the translation!

Translating the activities

Let's look at what some of the jargon means.

- **Analysing** – picking apart to find the meaning. This is expanded upon further on in this section.

- **Deploying different research techniques** – this simply means using different ways of finding information.

- **Evaluating** – judging whether something does effectively what it sets out to do. This is also explained in more detail further on.

- **Synthesising** – this means bringing together discrete or separate items of information and ideas from different texts or parts of a text, usually so that you can present a complete picture or body of evidence or information. It's the opposite of analysing.

- **Analysing linguistic devices and techniques** – this includes understanding and explaining a writer's use (effectively and imaginatively) of appropriate figures of speech, imagery, repetition, rhetorical questions, word-choice and the like.

- **Texts** – these are materials and resources, mainly written ones. The kind of texts you will read and study include many or most of the following types: reference texts, including print and electronic texts; reports; extended factual articles from journalistic texts; extended news articles and broadcast news items/reports; documentary broadcasts; feature articles and documentaries dealing with different points of view; persuasive texts including advertisements; biography and autobiography; letters and memoirs; formal essays; literary texts from different genres.

DEFINING TEXTS IN MORE DETAIL

A 'text' is wider in meaning than you might think. Take it to include books, extracts from books, websites and graphic or picture material. Electronic texts could include CD–ROMs and disc contents. So, a 'text' is anything that can be 'read', in the widest sense of the word.

- **Reference texts** – include the obvious, like dictionaries and encyclopaedias, but also every other kind of writing that you will find in the reference section of your library. Go to the library and spend some time looking at the amazing range of reference books that are on the shelves there. Similarly, look at the range of materials available to you on the Internet and on disc.

- **Journalistic texts** – are lengthy articles in the serious press, including magazines. It *doesn't* mean articles from the tabloids*. The average reading age of daily tabloids is 8 years, so they are not included in Higher English. Read the broadsheets* for the purposes of developing interpretation skills. There's no harm in your reading about the lives of pop-stars, television 'personalities' and film babes if that appeals to you, but it won't really help a lot with what we're talking about at the moment.

- **Broadcast texts** – can also be 'read'. The term covers both radio and television broadcasting, but includes only factual material, such as documentaries, news and topical issues coverage. It *excludes* soaps, dramas and films, though a very good case could be made for including them.

- **Persuasive texts** – are designed to *persuade* you to adopt a point of view other than the one you probably started with. Note that this includes advertising, whose whole purpose is just that. These are particularly good for study when we are trying to examine the craft of the writer.

- **Letters** – the letters that you will come across in Higher English are unusual. They have been written almost always with an eye towards their eventual publication and are far more detailed and 'literary' than a letter to a friend, for example.

- **Essays** – are conscious examples of a particular literary form. Think of those you will find in published collections, George Orwell's essays, for example.

- **Literary texts** – imaginative literature of different types (genres*). These include prose, poetry, and drama. We've already covered another genre in our discussion of other texts, non-fiction.

- **Purpose** – you will be reading each text with a particular **purpose** in mind. You will be thinking about the writer's purpose when you are reading. You will have your own purpose when you write.

Performance criteria

Now let's see how well you have to do the activities in order to succeed in the unit. The performance criteria are the descriptions of the work produced for assessment that reaches the pass-mark for an outcome of the unit. These are provided in the *Arrangements* for the use of your teachers in assessing your work. You can use them as targets to aim at or to surpass. It's necessary to quote the *Arrangements* in full here.

> *Acceptable performance in this unit will be the satisfactory achievement of the standards set out in this part of the unit specification. All sections of the statement of standards are mandatory and cannot be altered without reference to the Scottish Qualifications Authority.*
> *[A reminder of Outcome 1:]*
> ### Outcome 1
> *Understand, analyse and evaluate non-fiction print text which conveys complex information.*
> ### Performance criteria *[for Outcome 1]*
> Understanding
> *Responses demonstrate understanding of significant ideas / information and supporting details, provide explanation of their relationships and summarise adequately the main concerns of the text (or part of the text).*
>
> Analysis
> *Responses explain accurately and in detail ways in which aspects of structure / style / language contribute to meaning / effect / impact.*

Evaluation

An evaluation is made of the effectiveness of the text which takes into account the writer's purpose(s) and stance, makes appropriate use of critical terminology and is substantiated with detailed and relevant evidence from the text.

Translating the performance criteria

How does that translate? 'Acceptable performance' for this outcome means achieving 50% in the end-of-unit test.

The next item, the outcome, you've seen before. It simply states that you have to show that you can answer questions on a piece of writing about factual matters (i.e. not fiction or other literature) which includes quite difficult ideas.

As you can see, there are three parts to the performance criteria:

1   understanding

2   analysing

3   evaluating.

We'll take them one at a time.

1 Understanding

Questions on understanding will ask you about *meaning*. You are expected to explain what the writer means when he or she writes certain things. The difficulty arises because the writer will use language both literally and figuratively; there will be explicit and implicit meaning; there will be ambiguity and reference; there will be inference and suggestion; there will be irony and, hardest of all for students to recognise it seems, the writer might even use humour. Whatever the writer does will be for his or her own writing *purpose*. By answering the examiner's questions you must show that you understand the purpose.

This understanding does not just mean that you have to know the dictionary definition of words selected from the text. It also involves comprehension of the meaning of words, descriptors, qualifiers, modifications, and of the tone and stance of the writer. You have to comprehend the writer's purpose, what his views are, what his ideas are about and what he wants to communicate to you by way of this piece of writing. And you have to be able to express all this in your own writing.

You will be asked questions about the meaning of words, phrases, and whole statements. Some will ask about the meaning in context, some in isolation. They will usually ask you also to explain *how* you know or understand. That kind of question attracts as many marks as the earlier part of the question about the actual meaning. There will also be questions about the meaning of whole ideas and also concerning the whole text. A common way of ascertaining your understanding is to invite you to write an extended answer or even a short summary of at least part of the text.

2 Analysing

Analysis is like deconstruction – taking things apart carefully so that when you put them back together again, the thing still works as it did before you started the analysis.

For our purposes, in the close reading requirements, analysis questions ask you to describe how the writer has put together the message of the text, with its ideas and style. The questions deal with the structure and sequencing of the piece of writing. This is completely different from those questions that ask about meaning.

Questions on structure are always very badly answered in examinations. The reason for this is that students read the questions and fail to recognise them as questions about analysis. They seem always to read them as if they were saying, in effect 'What does this sentence mean?' when, actually, they are saying something like 'How does the writer's idea in paragraph 1 connect with a similar idea in paragraph 2?'

One way to help deal with questions that are designed to ask you how the writing works is to think of the piece of writing as something that the writer has made. Think of it in the same way as you would think of, for example, a chair that has been made by a craftsperson. A question about meaning would ask 'What is a chair?' Analysis is concerned with how the chair functions? How is it held together? What does one particular part contribute to the whole structure? The analysis questions are all dealing with *how*.

Don't get carried away by what the writer says, and forget to look carefully at *how* he or she says it. You must try to show *how* the writer uses the structure, the style and the choice of language to convey meaning – don't just concentrate on the literal meaning of the words.

3 Evaluating

When you come to evaluate a piece of writing, the questions will direct you to particular aspects or parts of the text and ask your *opinion*. This is where you must show your involvement and interest in the piece you have been reading. What if you didn't like it and weren't remotely interested in it?

That in itself is an opinion. Remember that criticism is a neutral not a negative word. An adverse opinion is acceptable, but you must be able to back up what you have to say by using examples or evidence from the text. In fact, it is probably easier to be positive.

The person carrying out your assessment will be keen to learn what *you* thought of the material. Remember always to address the point of the question, but also say how the writing caught your attention and how the use of particular features (vocabulary, style, tone, mood, setting, ideas, argument, for example) helped to make the writing more effective for you. Back up what you say by quoting or referring to words or phrases that convinced you. Often questions of this kind invite a longer response, but always look for guidance in the wording of the question and in the mark allocation.

Evidence requirements

The next part of the *Arrangements* document, describes for your teachers the kind of evidence they must have of your progress in close reading.

> *Written or spoken responses to unseen questions on an unseen non-fiction text which conveys complex information.*
>
> *Responses must be unassisted and written or spoken in the presenting centre under supervision.*
>
> *The text will be characterised by: content which communicates information, ideas and meaning at a sophisticated level (often marked by the number and relationship of ideas, by the density of detail or by abstraction); consistent and varied use of paragraphs to support line of thought and structure; varied use of sentence structure; apposite choice and skilful use of words.*

Translation of evidence requirements

- **Spoken responses** – unfortunately a spoken response does not produce retainable evidence of the kind that would be required in the event of an appeal. Don't choose to present your work in this way if you can avoid it.

- **Supervision** – the unit assessment is different from an external examination, but may not seem like it. You will probably sit a NAB test in the classroom or hall. It will be run like an examination, but without external invigilators. There will be a time limit of about one hour. Your teacher or another teacher will administer it and mark it also.

- *Text* – the description of the text here is rather scary. However, the text will look very much like that presented on every other Higher English close reading paper. The questioning will be minimally different in scope from the external examination, but the form of the questions will be similar. In order to pass this particular outcome, you must score a minimum of 50% of the available marks. Aim higher, though.

Assessment of close reading

As we have seen, direct assessment of close reading is by an internal end-of-unit assessment or test which is marked by a teacher from your school. There is no assessment of close reading via the folio, but it will feature in the external examination at the end of the course.

This is not to say that you won't cover interpretation skills during your course and as part of your coursework. You will be taught how to respond to passages of prose: how to understand, analyse and evaluate them. And, of course, you will get the chance to practise on past examples of interpretation passages.

CHAPTER FIVE

THE LANGUAGE STUDIES UNIT: WRITING

Writing: Language Studies Unit Outcome 2

We're now looking at the second part, Outcome 2, of the Language Studies Unit. You already know that you will be covering Outcome 2, writing, at the same time as the first outcome (close reading) and, indeed, at the same time as the other course units still to be discussed.

What the *Arrangements* say

Just as they did for Outcome 1 (close reading), the *Arrangements* tell us what you have to be able to do at the end of the unit for Outcome 2. The outcome is to produce a particular kind of writing:

> *Compose a piece of writing in a particular genre*

So we know that this part of the unit is where you are going to be involved in activities to improve your writing skills. You might be wondering which 'particular genre' you are expected to write. Here 'genre' means no more than 'kind', 'form' or 'type' of text.

Activities

So, in this part of the unit you will write many pieces of text, of different kinds (look at the list of activities and texts printed earlier in connection with Outcome 1, pages 28 and 29). For the unit *assessment*, you have to produce only **one** piece of writing of a particular kind. For the outcome, you will choose what kind of writing you will compose or produce and write one example, which will go in your folio.

Choosing a genre

You have to produce only one piece of writing for your folio to address this outcome, but there are many genres. So you have a choice. As you cover this unit, you will deal with several different kinds of writing, which will bring you into a position to make your choice. Your choice will be based on what you can do best. Maybe you already know what kind of writing you do best, but by the end of the unit you certainly should. For that reason, we'll look now at the classroom activities you can expect to take part in to prepare you to meet the outcome successfully.

If you look back to the earlier list of activities (page 28), you'll see that the activities that are *not highlighted* have to do with *composing your own writing* as opposed to understanding, analysing and evaluating someone else's. As you use texts by other people to study for understanding, analysis and evaluation, you will learn what they mean, how they were composed, and how to say what you think of them. You will also use them as models for your own writing. That doesn't mean that you will simply copy them. No. Studying many texts opens up the range of what's possible, shows what can be done, and provides ideas, systems, structures, expressions and so on. When you can see *how* they've been crafted, you can use them to help you to create your own writings. Texts produced by others show you what to do and what not to do. Being good at analysing or deconstructng texts also allows us to construct our own ideas and expressions into writing that 'works'.

You have three choices for the writing outcome:

1   expressive writing

2   creative writing

3   a report.

You can see from the list of texts for the unit already set out for close reading that your course will deal not only with the kind of writing that you will choose to do. The course has to meet the needs of the whole class group and the individuals within it, you included. It also has to expose you individually to many different forms. There will be many different choices, because you and your classmates will choose different kinds of writing. You'll be choosing at the end to compose the kind (genre) you're best at. If you don't know this already, you're certain to find out from your teacher which form it is. If your teacher isn't telling you (very unlikely) . . . ask and discuss it.

We'll look at the three broad categories of writing in turn. These three categories do not cover all the kinds of writing that there are – just those that can be sampled in the assessment. For that reason, you'll find that they get more attention in the course. If it's to be assessed, it will be taught. If it's not in the assessment package, it will be neglected!

Expressive writing

This kind of writing includes several different types within it:

- reflective writing

- persuasive writing

- argumentative writing.

A note about writing in Scots

When you come to the Literary Studies Unit a little further on (Chapter 6), you will be reminded that at least one of the texts that you study *must* be a Scottish text. It's entirely possible that you are not Scots and have no knowledge of Scots language or literature. The definition of Scottish literature is quite loose, however, and is so inclusive that it presents no problems.

It is useful to note here that there are opportunities for you to *write* in Scots also, particularly in imaginative writing. My special note is to encourage you to take up this opportunity and produce work in Scots. Your reading of literary texts written in Scots will help you here, and so will the spoken language of Scots speakers.

Reflective writing

Reflective writing is a fairly sophisticated form of text. It is written to interest and please the reader by making him or her think about the implications of an idea or experience. It's not simply about giving information. It is a description of how the writer processes a certain piece of information and learns from it. The writing is generated by reflecting on an idea or experience and by sharing with the reader the kind of thoughts or feelings the writer has about it now. A good example would be to recount or describe very concisely a single childhood experience and to share with the reader what you think about it now that you look back. The reflective part of the account is what is important. Writing about your childhood is a very popular form of writing with students, and it's usually a very good choice, too. Without reflection, however, it's autobiography and doesn't qualify as reflective writing. You wouldn't meet the requirements of the unit. If you produce a simple account of the incident without offering your *present* thoughts on the experience, you will fail.

Your teacher will have guidance to teachers on the reflective essay as part of the support pack for Higher English. He or she may even have some very good guidance offered years ago in connection with Creative Writing at CSYS (now called Advanced Higher) but this is still totally valid. Ask to see it.

Persuasive writing

The name for this kind of writing is fairly self-explanatory. Your purpose is to persuade the reader round to your point of view about a single topic. It might include the sort of writing that's used in advertising or to review a product or performance, for example. It is writing designed to change the mind or convince the reader to share your view. It is to be distinguished from argumentative writing (see below).

Argumentative writing

This kind of writing isn't as unpleasant as it might sound! 'Argue' is a word that has suffered a shift in meaning. It's not really about having a bad-tempered row with someone. An argument is actually the *body of evidence* put forward to support a particular case or view. So, argumentative writing is close to persuasive writing in this sense. The crucial requirement of argumentative writing is that it takes a topic or issue (let's say the tried and tested, weary case of school uniform) and presents the case *for and against*, leading on to the *conclusion* that the writer wishes to present to the reader. The school uniform argument would require you to include the main points in favour of it (usually reduction in bullying/feelings of inferiority/shared identity/school ethos etc.) as well as the main points against it (hopelessly out of fashion/enforcing childhood on young adults/removing choice and creativity, etc.). The writing would lead the reader to the writer's view through the writer's line of argument.

Incidentally, if you do choose to include argumentative writing in your folio for assessment by SQA, don't choose to write about this particular topic unless you have some **passionately-held and original beliefs** about it. The examiners are only human and, while they would treat your writing with all proper consideration, they deserve a break from topics they've read about many, many times before. They do know that it might be the first time YOU have written about it, of course.

Examiners won't mark you down for your choice of a hackneyed * subject, as long as you show imagination, originality, independent thought and creativity. Examiners, like anyone else, get bored. Remember this when you choose a subject for your writing.

As well as the tried and tested, weary topics, there are those that are done to death because they are currently fashionable. Some topics, such as euthanasia, abortion, the rain forest, drug abuse and capital punishment are perhaps best avoided, unless you have extensive knowledge, clear ideas, a strong personal point of view and the ability to present a balanced argument.

Finally, a quick word about plagiarism. Don't be tempted to lift material directly from other sources. You could have your certificate cancelled in *all* your subjects. It's just not worth the risk.

Creative writing

This category includes kinds of writing that are probably already familiar to you. You have the opportunity to produce original creative pieces of writing:

- prose fiction – that is short stories or (extracts of) novels
- poems
- drama.

These are the kinds of literary work you have been reading since you started at school and will still be reading (and studying) in the Literary Studies Unit of the course. We'll be dealing with that unit later on in THE GUIDE. The works that you read for the Literary Studies Unit will help you as models for the writing tasks in this unit. Let's now look at the possibilities in the creative writing option.

Prose fiction

There are many kinds of writing that can be described as fiction, and it isn't easy to come up with a definition of what is and what isn't prose fiction. The most straightforward forms are the short story and the novel. It's unlikely that you are going to choose to write a novel – the length alone makes it an improbable choice. You could produce an *extract* from a novel, however, even if the rest of the novel doesn't exist. A short story isn't simply a story that happens to be short . . . a long short story could be longer than a short novel. That is a paradox*.

If you think you are going to concentrate eventually on the prose fiction, there are one or two things about this form of creative writing that you might like to bear in mind. The first and most obvious you will already know. We use the words 'fact' and 'fiction' as opposites. So prose fiction is not factual writing. It is the work of the imagination. Everyone knows that all fiction is based on some factual situation. Fiction is processed by the imagination of the writer, however, from its factual origins. Straight recounting of factual events is not fiction. There is a form called 'faction'. Truman Capote's *In Cold Blood*, a classic of this form, is a good example. It's an account of a real mass murder, but written in the form of a novel with unmistakable reality intruding.

The boundaries between different forms are increasingly blurred these days. The hard and fast rules that used to define works of literature into categories or genres have been eroded by experimentation and creativity. However, for your purposes, a piece of prose fiction can be described as follows:

- It must be written in prose, obviously.

- There must be a plot (or narrative or story line), and characters that you create.

- There must be a beginning, a middle and an end (not necessarily in that order, but in the form of an opening, a development and a conclusion).

- There must be a suitable structure, style and form so that we know it is prose fiction.

- The reader must be able to see that you have carefully selected and controlled your writing so that it contains what it should, and leaves out irrelevant material.

- The writing must use language purposefully, to create tone, mood, atmosphere. It should employ imagery, symbolism and dialogue.

- You, the writer, should make your presence felt in the writing. The reader should recognise your stance in the fiction.

Most of these features are mentioned in the *Arrangements*. There is one final point to be added to the description of prose fiction.

- It should be *your own creation*.

We have already mentioned the dangers of plagiarism. They apply here also – don't do it!

Choosing a subject of fiction

The subject of your fiction is your own choice, and the choice is infinite. You can think of themes and topics as the setting for your creative writing. For example, any of these might be the subject of a piece of fiction:

- a recent experience or issue

- an obsession or a prejudice

- a memory or sudden thought

- an event or relationship*

- a misunderstanding or argument

- an event or an activity.

Poetry

Writing poetry is, sadly, regarded as a minority activity – particularly so if the end-product is going to be assessed. Some people think that poetry is so subjective, such an individual matter, that it can't be assessed at all. One of the major problems in making this your choice for the piece of creative writing is that you are unlikely to be taught about writing poetry to anything like the extent that you will be taught prose writing. Another consideration is that it has to be a brave soul who puts all their eggs in the poetry basket, so to speak: a short poem, in particular, doesn't provide enough opportunities for you to demonstrate that you can fulfill all the requirements for the outcome. Unless you already know *and your teacher agrees* that you are capable of writing poetry of the quality required, you would be best advised to avoid it and choose one of the other options available to you. That is a very disappointing thing to have to say, especially since the examiners complain annually of how little poetry appears.

If you are contemplating submitting a poem or set of poems despite the difficulties I have mentioned, you should take note of some important features of good poetry. Poetry is very different from prose: in its use of heightened language; in the deliberate choice of words; in the way they are arranged and in the use of verses (or stanzas as they are often called). Poetry uses unusual connections between words. Its ideas are concise and condensed usually, with much figurative language as the norm. It plays with sound and rhythm, with unusual ideas, imagery and syntax*. Whatever its topic, a poem should be presented with originality and with deliberate impact. The poem needs to be closely focused: there should be a strong sense of unity about the piece, and the writer's engagement with the topic should be clear. While there are many forms that the poem might take, and many free forms also that could be offered, a poem is *not* just prose chopped up into manageable lengths.

If poetry is a creative writing form that appeals to you, and your teacher agrees that you have the capability and precision of ideas required, you should certainly go for it. Consider hedging your bets by offering a set of poems linked by a common theme. You increase the assessment opportunities by submitting more work. If you do this, however, the advice you need is to limit very strictly the number of pieces – three is plenty. More than that almost certainly means that the thoughts are more diffuse than is good for the purpose, and some of the pieces will show their weaknesses more readily.

Choosing a subject for poetry

The topics for poetry are, of course, your own choice, from a range as wide as for prose. Many of the topics or themes offered as ideas there (pages 38 and 39) apply also to poetry. In addition, consider:

- a person or a place
- an experience or activity
- an idea or an image
- a relationship or situation.

Dramatic script

A third option for assessment of creative writing is to offer a dramatic script. You should learn quite a bit about written drama during the course. You will certainly be reading drama as part of the Literary Studies Unit, and you may already have read plays for the stage and television, for radio and film in your studies so far. You will also have watched or listened to dramatic performances as well, in any of these media. However, we are concerned here with *writing* dramatic script. The reason for mentioning the *performance* aspect of this writing is to remind you that such a script will be successful only if it can be performed in some way. Drama writing is not simply for reading on the page. The writing has to indicate sensibly how the drama might be produced and performed.

A particular feature of drama writing is one you cannot fail to have observed when you have been reading it: the meaning is brought to you almost exclusively by the *spoken* words of the characters. There is not a great deal of room for expanded story-telling by the dramatist speaking directly to the reader, although some dramatists favoured this notion: George Bernard Shaw, for example. He could go on at considerable length telling us about characterisation. On the other hand, notice how little Shakespeare has to say to the reader in stage directions or character sketches. His celebrated '*Exit, pursued by a bear*' is one of his lengthier contributions.

It is unlikely, especially for assessment purposes, that you are going to produce a complete three-act play for stage or television: more likely that you will offer a single scene (once again, a scene or extract from an otherwise non-existent whole play is acceptable), a sketch, or perhaps a monologue*. (If you are unfamiliar with this form of writing, have a look for the humorous and satirical monologues of, for example, Alan Bennett, either in print or on tape.)

To produce a convincing dramatic script, you must be able to create characters that your reader can believe in and whose ideas and feelings they can share. Your main method of communication with your readers will be dialogue – the actual words of the characters you are building – but brief stage directions can say much about movement, bearing, body-language. A drama of any kind must have a setting, and you have to establish this. The characters and setting will exist against the background of a theme, and your writing will set up a particular atmosphere or mood. It might be mystery, humour, fear, tension, expectation or horror, for example.

Obviously, dramatic writing has a characteristic layout and appearance on the page, and you must show that you have mastered the form. The model plays that you study will help you. So, you see that this kind of writing is not just a matter of telling a story in a form different from prose fiction. You can see that, in drama, there are *constraints* that the fiction writer does not face. If you choose to write a dramatic script for assessment purposes, make sure that you have consulted your teacher about whether this is your best option. Again, the simple rule is to find out during the course which of the forms is clearly your best and to go for it. If you happen to be one of those lucky people who can with genius do almost anything you turn your hand to, then you won't have any problems in choosing. Unfortunately, very few of us are like that, so choosing is a matter of practice, experience and taking the best advice you can get. In the course, the person best placed to advise you on your best work is the person assessing it. For Unit assessment in the NQ course, that person is your teacher.

Report writing

As one of the various forms of writing you will experience in the course, and in this unit in particular, report writing is something of an odd man out.

Report writing is a valuable skill, some say an essential skill in the modern world. Every course will, no doubt, include it in the teaching, and you should certainly be learning how to do it. As a choice for your assessment piece, however, there is a problem. A report is based on the writer's judgement of a series of source materials. As part of the unit assessment there ought to be an assessment of how well the source materials were understood, condensed, sequenced and expressed in the report. However, if you chose this option for your folio assessment the examiner does not have access to your source materials, and the report is assessed purely for its writing qualities, without being compared to the materials being reported on. At SQA, it looks like a report, right enough, but there's no way of telling whether it reports appropriately on the sources on which it is based.

So, it might be better not to choose this option for assessment, but don't neglect it as a skill that you should be learning in the course.

Standards of performance (Language Studies Unit)

The standards of performance are a quick summary to give you an understanding of what your work must be like for you to pass, or 'achieve the outcome' in jargon.

> The standards of performance are the minimum levels of attainment. Don't aim for this as your best. Aim always to do better . . . the best you can.

These standards, taken from the *Arrangements*, will, of course, apply to both the internal and external assessment of the piece that is sent to SQA in your folio.

Writing

Content

Content is relevant and appropriate for purpose and audience, reveals depth and complexity of thought and is fully developed.

Structure

Structure is effective and appropriate for purpose, audience and genre: content is sequenced and organised in ways which assist impact.

Expression

Capable use of techniques relevant to the genre and effective choice of words and sentence structures sustain a style and tone which clearly communicate a point of view/stance consistent with purpose and audience.

Technical accuracy

Spelling, syntax and punctuation are consistently accurate.

Note: according to purpose, content is likely to be reflection, ideas, opinion, argument, information.

CHAPTER SIX

THE LITERARY STUDIES UNIT

The place of literature in Higher English and in life

This unit is actually covered in a mere five pages in the *Arrangements* document, and even that includes the inevitable *Arrangements*-style lists and a degree of repetition. This apparently brief entry belies* its importance in the course, however.

Literature is of central importance to the whole course. Indeed, English teaching is based on the study of literature, and all aspects of language study are related to it. This is hardly surprising when you think about it. The works of literature that we study are examples of the finest use of our language and of the creative imagination. We study them to derive enjoyment, of course, but also to learn from them: how to read, how to write, to provide vehicles for talk and listening, and to develop our grasp of language. They give us scope for imaginative thinking, and enable us to share the experiences of others, real and imaginary. In this way, they provide us with what has been described as *vicarious experience*. This is not our own experience, but is so absorbingly brought to us that we cannot help but share it with the writer, as if it were our own. This is how we can empathise with the feelings and emotions of fictional characters and how we can believe in their experiences, their happiness and their disasters. Much of this actually helps us to make sense of our own lives and we benefit from it.

This week, for example, I have been reading five different books. Their worlds were all very different from any of ours: a life or death adventure in the Aegean during the Second World War (*Guns of Navarone* by Alistair MacLean); a black and hilarious set of confusions and mishaps in New York and Alabama (*Stars and Bars* by William Boyd); an episodic multi-faceted view of the experiences of war from many sides (*The Young Lions* by Irwin Shaw); a taut and worrying hi-jack mixed with Aboriginal mysticism and Arab fanaticism (*Flying Hero Class* by Thomas Keneally); and an amazing account of endurance in a bid for freedom (*The Long Walk* by Slavomir Rawicz). Apart from the last, these are all works of fiction with at least one character or situation that has affected me in one way or another.

What have you been reading? How did it make you feel?

In the former East Berlin in the very ironically named Babelplatz, there is a memorial which illustrates to us the potential power of literature, and the fear that this can provoke. You look down through a heavy glass panel set into the paving and see the strangest sight. It is a room below ground, completely white and utterly empty, except for the bookshelves that line all four walls. These are totally empty, with an emptiness that shrieks out significance. It is the memorial to a night in 1933 when the Nazis carried out an event that told the world what to expect. On this spot, in the public campus of the principal

43

university, the Humboldt University in the Unter den Linden, in the centre of Berlin, they set alight huge bonfires. They were burning books: books of ideas and philosophy, of imagination – books that they knew could affect the minds of the people who read them. The empty memorial, this mausoleum, is a striking symbol of the empty world they wished to create.

Consider this fear of the power of books. The Soviets, as well as the Nazis, methodically destroyed and banned the literature and culture of the European countries they occupied. They knew that the books could inspire people to resistance and survival against military power. We see the same thing in Afghanistan under the Taliban; in Cambodia under the Khmer Rouge. They even killed people who wore glasses, because they were obviously readers. In Soviet Russia, people struggled to publish illegally under pain of exile and death in Siberia the *samizdat*, the works run off in back rooms and cellars on primitive mimeograph presses. Nearer home, the Gaelic language and its literature were suppressed, even in the schools. At a less exalted level, until recent times, the great cities of the Soviet Union, such as Moscow and Leningrad, did not even publish a residential numbers telephone directory. That's not literature, of course, but the suppression showed the power of the printed word and communication.

What this tells us is that literature has great power in the minds of those who read it. You should work hard to gain some of that power. It is one of the reasons for studying literature.

The study of literature

The work in this unit will be fairly familiar territory for you if you've already done Standard Grade English, but there are some very clear differences apart from the level of performance that's expected at Higher.

The outcome

We'll look at what you will be doing in the way of classroom activities during the course, but first, the quick way of summing this up is to look at the outcomes.

There is a single outcome for this unit:

> *Respond critically to imaginative texts.*

This is a rather bald statement and I will expand on it, but not at great length.

Evidence requirements

In the unit assessment you are expected to produce what, in Standard Grade terms, was called Critical Evaluation of Literature (CELs), dealing with works that you have studied in class. There are some differences, naturally. The standard of work demanded at Higher is a major advance on Standard Grade. The actual details of what you are to produce for internal assessment also differ.

For Higher, you will write **two** pieces of critical work on literature that you have studied in class. There are certain limited choices that you can make in fulfilling this requirement.

You can submit either:

- **two** critical essays, each in response to an unseen question on a previously studied text or texts.

or

- **one** critical essay as above, **and** one textual analysis.

There are some restrictions and some concessions which qualify the choice you can make:

1   The texts that you write about will be drawn from the four genres; prose, poetry, drama and mass media.

2   If you choose to write the two critical essays, they must each deal with a different genre.

3   At least one of the texts that you choose to write about must be a Scottish text (the definition of an acceptable Scottish text is given below). (page 48)

4   You must not write about any text that is also the subject of your specialist study (see Chapter 8).

5   There are no mandatory word limits indicated for the critical essay, neither minimum nor maximum.

6   You must meet all the criteria for the assessment of each critical essay (or textual analysis) on its assessment occasion. (These criteria follow below.)

7   The assessments for the two items will take place on two separate occasions.

Critical essay and textual analysis

These two terms need very brief explanations. They are two different ways of responding to literature, and for you, they each have some advantages and disadvantages.

The critical essay is straightforward. It's an essay in which you criticise a *text that you have studied closely*. The essay is written in response to a specific question that will be put to you in the assessment, and it will be your task to take into account the features of the text that are relevant to the question. The important thing here is that you choose from a range of questions about texts from each of the four genres, and provide the structure of the essay for yourself. You take into account the key ideas and particular features of the work.

Textual analysis is the same as what used to be called practical criticism. It consists of an *unseen* and (normally) short text, perhaps a poem or extract from a longer prose or dramatic text, followed by questions. These questions invite answers on the literary qualities of the text. What makes this different (from the critical essay) as an approach to literature is that you are not dependent on what you have learned about a particular text:

you are working independently, using what skills you have developed for the criticism and evaluation of literature in general. The other difference is that the questions provide a structure for your response, as if they are nudging you to remind you of the next thing to deal with. A little consideration here is the thought that markers mark positively, as I've said before. This means that they try to give credit where it can be found. Often it means that you gain the benefit of the doubt for each question, and this tends to be to your overall advantage, since all the little pluses add up.

You will be given advice by your teacher about which approach to adopt, and that advice will be reflected in his or her teaching. It is likely to be one or the other: critical essay or textual analysis. So, for many students, there won't be a choice at all.

> Please take the advice in the warning boxes below. Do not choose textual analysis if you haven't been taught how to do it.

Choosing a text

You will almost certainly opt for the prose genre, if you are like the majority of students. Here you will be able to choose to write about novels, short stories or a number of other literary forms, such as autobiography, memoirs, diaries, and essays. When tackling these forms in particular, it is as well to remember that the purpose of a critical essay is *never* simply to recount the plot or narrative structure of the work. That will lead to outright failure, as it will in the critical essay in the external examination and also in the Folio, where you will submit a specialist study of a work of your choice. In the choice of a prose work, that disastrous course of action is more tempting and more probable unless you are warned well off it. The story is probably the most memorable aspect of a prose work, especially in the novel and short story forms. Actually, this is only one minor feature of the work, as far as a critical essay is concerned.

As for the other genres, it is a pity that rather few students currently opt for poetry or drama texts. Certainly, these forms of literature make greater demands on your critical skills. They tend not to have the overwhelming narrative features of prose works. This means that you must focus on the linguistic techniques and devices used by the poet or dramatist. Poetry offers a compact text to write about, making a poem a very good choice once you have the skills to analyse it. We'll be mentioning these skills when we look at the activities and performance criteria associated with this unit.

At the present time only about 4% of students attempt mass media texts, and many of those who do, do so in despair.

1   Absolutely *do not* attempt to write about any media text if the study of these texts has not been a major part of your course.

2   The standard required in writing about media texts is the same as for the other genres. Don't think that they present an easy option. They don't.

3   If you do decide that the mass media option is for you, read the information and
     advice on the literary genres as if they were for the media. The two genres are very
     similar.

Choosing genres

If you choose the two-essay option in this unit, you must write about *two different works in
two different genres*. It's probable that your unit assessment will take place over two
occasions and that you'll do one critical essay each time. So you'll have to remember
which genre you chose on the previous occasion. Some teachers may go for an assessment
covering both essays at the same time. This is unlikely, because of the time available for
unit assessment.

> **Warning**
>
> It's very important to keep to this rule of selecting a different genre for each essay. If you write
> on the same genre for both, one of the pieces earns no credit whatsoever. You would simply
> have to make another attempt at the assessment. Remember that you are normally allowed
> only a single re-assessment.
>
> There is another important exclusion concerning the genre of the text you choose to write
> about. It is not acceptable to write about the same text(s) in different parts of the assessment.
> So, you must write about different texts in the unit assessment, the external examination and
>   in the specialist study.

> **Warning**
>
> I'll mention this matter again further on, in the external exam section dealing with the critical
> essay, where there is a similar exclusion. Since there is only one critical essay to be written in
> the external exam, it's not a question of writing about different genres, as in the unit. It is
> about dealing with the genre that is specified in the question. Fortunately, in the exam the
> genre questions are in separate headed sections, so it's harder to make the mistake of writing
> about poetry when the question is about drama, for example. Nevertheless, every year quite a
> few students manage to do this in the external examination, and lose major numbers of marks
>   for their trouble. So be careful about this.

Covering a Scottish text

It's not necessary to issue a warning as above about the Scottish text requirement. Any
assessment in the unit will automatically include questions on a Scottish text, because it is
compulsory for you to have studied at least one in this unit. This means that, if you choose
the two-essay option, then one of these will be the Scottish text, naturally. If you choose
the critical essay and textual analysis option, then likewise, either the text you choose for
the critical essay, or the text basis for the textual analysis must be a Scottish text. The NAB

material used for the unit assessments will cater for this requirement by offering critical essay choices based on Scottish texts as well as non-Scottish texts, and also textual analysis choices based on both kinds of text.

> **Warning**
>
> You should make it your own responsibility to ensure that you have got the correct combination of items (whether two critical essays, or critical essay and textual analysis) completed by the end of the unit. Make absolutely sure by asking and seeking clear assurance that you have completed the outcomes for assessment in this unit. If you omit the Scottish text-based item in this unit, you will fail.

Definition of a Scottish text

Although it will, in practice, be up to your teacher to give you, or seek for you, clear advice about whether or not a text that you might choose is acceptable as a Scottish text, it's just as well for you to see the definition for yourself.

> *A Scottish text is defined for the purposes of this Literary Studies Unit as one that deals with issues of life or experience in Scotland and/or is the work of a Scottish writer, whether or not resident in Scotland.*
>
> *A media text for the same purpose should be recognisably Scottish in subject matter and/or production and/or literary authorship and/or locale.*

Uileamh MacShakespeare

Neither of these definitions is what could be called tight. Notice that they do not insist even that the text be written in Scots. This means that many a text will be offered in the critical essay that has what many people would call a very tenuous grip on Scottishness. It does look as if the well-known 'Scottish Play', *Macbeth* by that famous Caledonian writer Uileamh MacShakespeare fits in here.

Since your teacher will choose the texts that you will study in the unit, and since he or she will be able to decide whether the text qualifies, you should not have too many concerns on that count.

For some students, this information will come as a great relief: for others it will be a great disappointment that the Scottish text might well be one whose connection with Scotland, and particularly with the language of Scotland, is hard to trace. My personal view is that this is an opportunity lost . . . but that's just my personal view.

Length of your criticism

The *Arrangements* do not make any statement about the expected length of the critical essays so there are no penalties for great length or evident brevity – for those features alone, that is. You should be aware, however, that there is no need to extend any essay beyond the point at which you have said all there is to be said. The task is to make sure that you have more than adequately (in terms of quality, not quantity) met the demands of the criteria in each essay, and then stop. Going on further leads to the dangers of repetition, digression and irrelevance. Instead of leading to more credit, these flaws can all spell failure.

Assessment

You will take a test to assess your skills and abilities in the requirements of this unit at some stage towards the end of the unit. On this occasion you will write the critical essay(s) and/or the textual analysis. The material you face will almost certainly be a NAB assessment instrument produced centrally and issued to your school for this specific purpose. You will probably have decided before you even see the test material which texts you have studied carefully and well enough to write about in the way required. The *Arrangements* leave some discretion to teachers about exactly how the assessment will be managed. Some will want you to do both pieces on a single occasion: others will set up separate assessment times for each essay/textual analysis. About an hour is suggested as the time for each of the essays, and about 45 minutes for the textual analysis.

Since, in the unit assessment, you will have to produce two essays (or one essay plus a textual analysis), there is not a major difference between the assessment instrument for the unit and the external examination question paper. There you will tackle one critical essay and one textual analysis; the actual tasks will look very similar. This means that you can seek out past question papers or specimen papers. Even the old Higher papers, up to 2001, will show you suitable questions, though not actual layout. You will find a specimen of a Higher Still-type paper in THE GUIDE (Chapter 11), but you can also find it at the time of writing on the SQA website (www.sqa.org.uk). There is no guarantee, however, that the website will carry this material in the future at the time when you are reading THE GUIDE.

Look at the paper. For the critical essay, you can see the genre categories and the typical questions. These you answer in terms of the texts that you have studied in class. For the textual analysis, there is the text itself, followed by the questions. The text is previously unseen, and the questions are structured to take you through the text, addressing the various literary features that it exhibits.

Try doing the sample paper. Perhaps this will help you to decide on your choice for the internally-assessed unit: two-essay version or the one-essay plus one-analysis version. Remember, of course, that the external exam reflects the skills learned in this unit, so the textual analysis is compulsory there.

Open book assessment

For the internal assessment you will be allowed to take in with you copies of the texts you have studied and intend to use as the basis for your essay(s). The purpose of this is to allow you to make quick reference for checking, quoting, etc. Not so that you can read the text for the first time during the exam!

There are rules about the details of this, but they are not complicated. You can take in with you the text (i.e. what the author wrote), and you can take such a text even if it has a critical introduction or notes. You may *not* take any book that is *purely a critical study* of the author's text. If you have studied a body of poetry, you may use the text if it is in a collection of that author's work; you may make a copy of your own of the works you have studied if they are in anthologies, various collections or editions. You can re-write the poem(s) or photo-copy them for yourself, but you have to have your teacher's advice about any possible copyright restrictions in that case.

Being able to take the text into the assessment is a wonderful advantage for most students. You don't *have* to have the text with you, but it really is very useful. It is highly motivating and reassuring. It also makes clear that the assessment is not about memorising texts. Examiners will, of course, expect much greater (perfect) accuracy in any quotations you make.

> **Tips on using quotations**
>
> Note that the correct word is 'quotation': not 'quote'. There is no such noun as 'a quote'.
>
> An associated fad that won't endear you to examiners is to write 'quote' at the start of a quotation and 'unquote' after it. Just use the inverted commas in your writing. The former was a useful device when journalists had to phone in their stories to typists at the newspaper/magazine office, a process that produced an amazing number of homophones* in print.

Performance criteria

When you come to write your critical essay(s) and/or textual analysis, there are again particular skill features to which you must pay attention. Three of these skills were covered in the Language Studies Unit, and there is one more which applies to this unit.

1 **Understanding** – your essay or analysis should make clear that you understand the key elements, the writer's central concerns and the important details of the text you are writing about.

2 **Analysis** – in the essay or analysis you must explain in detail and with accuracy some of the ways in which the author has used style, structure and language to make meaning, to create particular effects and give impact to the writing.

3 **Evaluation** – in what you write you must show how you react to the text. You must also comment on its effectiveness and support what you say with evidence from the text.

To these we now add:

4 **Expression** – in your essay/analysis, the structure, style and your use of language must make clear what you mean; you must keep to a line of thought that is always relevant to the purpose of your writing. You must be able to spell, punctuate and write grammatically, and also to use words/terms appropriate for criticism.

(There is a short list of such 'critical terminology' at the end of this section, (page 52) and you should make it your business to learn how to use these words. That does not mean just being able to define them as labels: it means actually using them with understanding.)

You might be wondering how on earth you are going to be able to do all this. Don't forget that all this assessment comes *after* the teaching. You'll get plenty of practice.

Activities

Let's look at the kind of work you will be doing in class to prepare for assessment, but also to provide you with the foundations of your education. Again remember that these activities do not take place in isolation in this unit. The rest of the course is going on alongside. The activities related to the study of literature will seem to take up a large proportion of the course, but they are designed to develop reading and many other skills that contribute to the other units of the course, as we've emphasised already. The activities will not be unfamiliar to you by this stage in your learning.

The activities will centre on the study of literary texts and will involve reading, writing, talking and listening:

■ Study of texts in class and individually.

■ Analysing effects and devices used in literature.

- Discussing ideas about the texts with others.

- Writing essays etc., setting out ideas about texts.

- Learning the ideas and concepts in criticism.

- Writing, using critical ideas and concepts.

As you can see, you will be consolidating the learning that you have become familiar with in the study of English up till this point and your work will be maturing.

The external examination is covered in more detail in Chapter 10.

Critical terminology

When you come to write about literary texts, you are expected to be familiar with words and expressions used in literary criticism. This means that you must be able to understand these words and expressions when you meet them in questions, as you will. It also means that you are expected to use them meaningfully when you write about texts. These words and expressions *include* the following, so you should make sure that you know them, and how to use them.

characterisation	conventions of genre
dialogue	syntax
structure	layout
word-choice	metaphor
tone	simile
narrative stance	personification
mood	imagery
sense of place	figurative language
techniques/devices	symbolism

CHAPTER SEVEN

THE ORAL COMMUNICATION UNIT

> **REMINDER**
>
> The advice and information here depends on the fact that you are being taught in the classroom. THE GUIDE cannot replace that essential basis. Your teacher is the central point of what you are doing in Higher English. This is about how to deliver what the assessment system demands of you.

Choices

In the unit on talking, there are theoretically three different choices for you:

- Individual presentation   (Unit 3a)
- Discussion   (Unit 3b)
- Critical listening   (Unit 3c)

I say 'theoretically' because, as I'm sure you've already found out if you're in a school or college, that choice is probably going to be made for you by the English Department, or

Oral Assessment

perhaps by the individual teacher. It is very unlikely that you will be given a free choice of how to tackle the oral requirement. This is because 'talking' and its assessment can be very time-consuming. It has to be internally assessed, for fairly obvious reasons, and it also has to be continuous.

Talking in Higher English and in life

It's important for you to understand the position of talking in your course and in your life in the real world outside of school.

We use different modes of language to communicate with each other and with ourselves. Talking is one of the two expressive modes: the other is writing. The receptive modes of language are reading and listening. Think about which of these you (and the rest of the population) uses most.

Talking is important in our lives, not only because it's our preferred communication linkage, but because we use it in preparation for the other modes of language. All the modes of language are interlinked, of course, but talking works as a kind of central channel for our contacts with other people.

There are still many people who believe that our education system should be based on reading and writing only. They believe that these are the true 'intellectual' systems, where the results can be seen and recorded. Somehow talking is seen as less demanding, less intellectual and less necessary in intelligent people. This is a curious idea if you extend it to skills and knowledge levels in all the subjects that you might go on to develop in the rest of your education and life.

Take a look at where this has led us in education in particular. It's the origin of that deplorable attitude to teaching and learning that is summed up by the expression commonly addressed to students: **'Sit down, shut up, and listen.'**

This is wonderfully satirised in Alexander Scott's not over-long poem entitled 'Scotch Education'. I quote it in full here:

> *Ah tellt ye. Ah tellt ye. Ah tellt ye.*

This approach does not recognise the importance of talking as the way in which we negotiate ideas. It is important to be able to talk through what we understand from reading and listening, and what we are going to write. We prepare ourselves for writing and reading and listening by talking things through. So, talking is a way of communicating, obviously, but it makes a major contribution to the other modes of language and vice versa. The language modes are interconnected, and it's very difficult to see them as separate from each other.

When we come to teach and learn skills, however, and also to assess those skills, we have to be able to concentrate on particular skills. It's artificial, of course, but necessary, to identify the skills separately so that we can say something about your attainment in each. This explains why, for the purposes of assessment and certification, we divide the course into separate units to some extent.

The 'shut up and listen' approach to learning and teaching has produced generations of Scots who are renowned as inarticulate. It used to be observed in university tutorials and seminars that Scots students had very little to say, in comparison with their fellow students from other countries. The explanation given for this was that Scots tended to speak when there was something worth saying: that the others tended to talk for the sake of talking. There was also an explanation offered that the ability to talk and articulate ideas was a class thing. We'll not go into that, other than to say it's not really credible as an explanation.

Fortunately, the days of that kind of approach to learning and teaching are over, and the requirements of Higher English reinforce that fact. The simple fact is that you have to bring your skills in talking up to the same level of competence as your skills in reading and writing. This requires:

- teaching
- learning
- practice
- motivation.

Individual presentation

Outcome

What you have to do here sounds very simple.

Deliver an oral presentation.

> **Note**
>
> Presentation is used instead of talk(ing) because some students will qualify by communicating in ways other than by talking. Deaf students might sign, for example.

When we expand on it, we see more clearly that the exact requirements are not so simple. Here are the requirements.

You must give an oral presentation (talk) that runs for five minutes (four minutes for Intermediate 2) to a small audience of at least three other people. The talk has to be done without any help from anyone else (no reminders or prompts from your teacher or classmates, for example). Your teacher will be quietly assessing your talk as you do this. You have to meet all the criteria (see below) in one talk. Your talk has to be planned and you must check with your teacher that you will be able to meet all the criteria in one go.

You have to keep a note of any sources you have consulted, and also retain any notes you use.

You don't have to answer questions from your audience as part of the assessment, although you might actually do that if you wish. Your teacher may have various videos from support material issued earlier. Ask if you can see them.

Performance criteria

Content of your presentation

- Your talk must have a clear purpose.
- What you say must fit the purpose.
- It must also be suited to the audience.
- Your ideas must have some depth.
- Your ideas must be complex (rather than simple).
- The content must be developed.

Structure of your talk

- Your talk must have a clear structure that you have planned.
- The structure should fit your purpose and the needs of the audience.
- What you have to say should be in a sensible sequence.
- You should organise your ideas so that your talk has impact on the audience.

Expression

- Your delivery must be clear and easily heard.
- You must use a style and tone that put across your point of view.
- Your style and tone must also fit your purpose and your audience.

Interaction with the audience

You must take into account the needs of your audience and respond to their reactions.

These criteria or judgement points will be used by your teacher to assess what you do in your talk. You should, therefore, study them very carefully so that you know what is expected of you. Now we'll look in more detail at some aspects of the criteria.

Content

The content of your talk has to be carefully thought through to make sure that it is the kind of talk that can help you to meet the criteria, since you have to show that you can manage all of them in the one talk. Don't be disheartened if you don't do too well in the early days of practice. You will be assessed towards the end of your studies in this unit. For most students, this will be towards the end of the course. I have already mentioned that the units will not take place one after the other in the way that they are set out in THE GUIDE and in the *Arrangements*, and you will have been developing your talk skills throughout the course. Assessment will follow the teaching and learning. You'll have had a lot of experience of talking before you're assessed. Indeed, if you've been in a school where Standard Grade talking has had a 'backwash effect', you'll already have much experience.

Discuss with your teacher the subject you would like to deal with in your talk, and make sure that it's going to be adequate in content. By content, I don't mean simple factual knowledge. I want to emphasise this point very much.

> **This unit is about talking skills. It's not a test of your general knowledge.**

It is entirely possible to fail to convince an expert in a particular subject but still to be a skilled speaker. So your teacher will *not* be testing you to find out how much you know about your subject. He or she should assess how well you talk about your subject.

In the past, some students were obliged to talk about some aspect of a novel, for example. So, while a student might talk about the character Atticus Finch in *To Kill a Mocking Bird* by Harper Lee, it was obvious that the teacher was the expert. The student knew much less than the teacher, and this was often reflected in the grade awarded. That was wrong. What was to be assessed was how well the student was able to talk about the subject chosen.

Where students chose their own topics, they were the experts. Teachers could concentrate on assessing students' talking skills. Students became skilful, confident speakers on subjects they knew very well.

The important point is that students can talk well and knowledgeably about their subjects when they chose them. However, we can't *ignore* the main content, which is the ideas and central message of what you have to say. Think about this when you choose your topic.

However, we can't *ignore* the main content, which is the ideas and central message of what you have to say. It's clear that you have to plan and consider carefully what you want to say.

According to the performance criteria, the ideas that you wish to communicate to your audience have to be complex and you must show that you have gone into the matter, whatever it is, in some depth. So a few simple ideas on your topic won't be enough. You must think carefully about the topic and come up with ways to take your analysis further. Though your talk might have only several points to be made, these points must be developed to a level that shows that there is depth in your thinking about the topic you have chosen. For each point, you will describe the basic idea; go on to explain clearly what the idea consists of; you will illustrate it with examples; you will introduce contrary aspects of the idea and take a firm line of approach; you will have a personal stance in relation to the idea and you will leave your listeners in no doubt that you have thought about the idea and formed a view. Also that you have expressed clearly the process you have been through.

Purpose

We have seen that all talks must have a purpose. Your purpose will be one of the following:

- to present information
- to present ideas
- to offer opinions.

If you aren't clear and firm about your purpose in talking, then it will show in your talk. The purpose is what binds your talk together.

Your purpose will be interconnected with the content and form of your talk: so you might choose in your talk to reflect on an experience (not the same as just recounting your experience); to set out ideas on your topic; to produce an argument (arguing the case for compulsory ID cards for under-21s, for example); to offer opinions on a particular issue that you feel strongly about (don't necessarily avoid politics, religion, sex, for example, in the belief that your teacher might not agree with you – you're being assessed on your talk skills). On the other hand, you might want to avoid contentious subjects like these by simply providing information about a topic on which you have specialised information, such as fashion, breeding guinea pigs, chart music.

Your must tailor your purpose and topic to fit your audience. If you happen to be the national champion in an unusual sport, such as epée, you have to remember that your audience will know very little about it and its technicalities. You must take account of that. It's the audience on that occasion that matters. It's their needs that you must consider. So your talk to your classmates on your specialised sport will be very different from the talk you are also giving to the Auchterteuchty Fencing Club.

Planning

In the same way, the structure of your talk must be thought through and planned so that it delivers what you want to say in the best possible way for the audience and for your purpose in talking on this occasion. You have to sit down and think of the plan for your delivery. Write down the headings for this plan: the ideas, the order in which you present them and what you have to say, including ideas for illustrations and examples, and repetitions for emphasis. The best plan is one that moves from the general ideas to the particular ideas and has a conclusion that draws these together. You have to think of how you can achieve the best impact. Your audience should be able to follow you step by step in a logical, organised sequence and at the end have a very clear idea of what your 'message' is. You have to plan your talk to make sure that this happens.

> **Tips for delivering a talk**
>
> You are giving a talk, not a rehearsed speech, delivered as if you were an actor speaking a learned script. If you do that, you'll certainly fail this unit. If you memorise word for word what you have to say, it's the same as writing the essay you had prepared for an exam without taking any account of the rubric* in the exam paper. You have to talk for the occasion: that means taking into account the entire situation at the moment you are giving the talk: the audience, their reactions, the room, the topical situation, if that's relevant on the day. Talking is not the same thing as making a speech as if to an unseen audience. If you approach it like a speech it will come over as a rehearsed and wooden, suiting the needs of no-one in particular.
>
> Similarly, talking is not the same as reading aloud. If you rely completely or even mainly on a written script, you will fail this unit just as surely. Reading aloud is a completely different skill, and it belongs among the reading skills not the talking skills, so don't even think of doing it.
>
> With both of these unacceptable forms of delivery, it is immediately clear to your audience (and your teacher/assessor) what you are doing, and demonstrates very clearly that you are not in command of what you have to say and how you are going to say it. It also shows them that you haven't really taken their needs into account . . . and that's one of the important criteria in this task.

Using notes and visual aids

You are allowed to make use of notes and of visual aids. Here are a few brief words about these.

Any notes you use in your talk should be brief – no more than headings – the kind of note that gives you a quick reminder of the next stage of your talk. You might not even need them once you've written them, and they should be no more than you could fit on a postcard, for example. If you're talking, you can't be reading anything more extensive at the same time. Get yourself into a frame of mind so that you know you are not going to need notes, but they're there just in case you want to have a quick glance at them now and again. This is a good test of your purpose and confidence in what you have to say. If you really know what you want to say, you probably won't need your notes. If you do use them, they have to be kept as part of the record of your internal assessment.

If you want to use visual aids (pictures, objects, OHTs*, for example) do so within reason. Too many images means you are getting into stage management, and have the additional task of having to co-ordinate the visuals with your talk. They have to be relevant and designed to illustrate your talk, and to take it forward. When I was teaching, a girl in my class asked was it okay to bring in her pet as a visual aid for her talk about it. Of course it was . . . until she turned up the next day with her horse! She did well. She had a helper outside the classroom window to hold the horse while she gave us all a lot of information about how to groom it.

A famous demonstration of the use of visual aids in a talk came from a training programme aimed at instructors for the US Army. It was done on film, and the speaker talked about how to assemble and dismantle a rifle. As he stood there with the rifle in his hands looking straight at the camera and the audience, there was a small box in the top right corner of the screen. It gradually grew bigger and bigger until the soldiers could see it was a girl sitting on the corner of a desk. She was swinging her long legs and doing her nails. While she was doing this, the instructor was rabbiting on about the rifle. Suddenly the small picture vanished . . . and the point was made. Nobody had been listening to the rifle talk. The 'visual aid' had been more interesting than the words. Some talks can be helped, others obliterated by the use of visuals.

Structure

We're moving now to the structure – the shape – of your talk. Your planning and your notes will reflect that structure. Obviously, you must have an introduction that tells the audience not only what your topic is, but also states your purpose. It might be quite simple, such as, stating what information you intend to give to the audience. So let's say for the sake of illustration that you have decided you are going to talk about the little-known island off the north coast of Scotland called Eilean nan Roan. I give this example because I'm pretty sure that no-one is going to choose that topic.

Your planned introduction is straightforward. It might be:

> *'I am going to talk about a very small island off the north coast of Scotland called Eilean nan Roan. Hardly anyone will have heard of it and I believe that there is a great deal of information about it that deserves to be better known.'*

This bog-standard introduction serves to provide your audience with two essential pieces of information: the topic and the purpose of your talk.

- To give information is the purpose.
- Eilean nan Roan is the topic.

However, this introduction is totally predictable, fails to attract the audience's attention in any dynamic way, and sounds rather dull. Your introduction might begin with some planned and arresting sentence, then moving to the purpose and topic:

> *'They left the family Bibles open on the kitchen tables and walked to the boats waiting to take them away from their homes for ever.*
> *Can you imagine what it would be like if that happened to you tomorrow?*
> *That's exactly what the people of Eilean nan Roan experienced. Eilean nan Roan is a 1 mile by 1 mile island off the north coast of Sutherland.*
> *I want to tell you about the event I started with, and to go on to explain why it happened and what were the consequences . . .'*

So, now you have an introduction with a purpose and a topic.

Eilean nan Roan

Next we have ideas to introduce and develop. I have chosen Eilean nan Roan as an example because it is simple as an illustration. There is a narrative structure that could be used for the talk: the setting, with perhaps a visual aid here, the way of life, difficulties, land ownership, the decision to leave, scattering of people, reflection on living on the edge compared with modern life in the cities, a conclusion with contemporary examples.

Not all subjects will have such an obvious structure built in. You have to make the structure by arranging your ideas and their development in a sensible sequence. That doesn't necessarily mean structuring your talk in the same way as the story in Alice in Wonderland, where the King of Hearts instructed the story-teller to:

> *'Begin at the beginning and go on till you come to the end: then stop.'*

There are many other sequences that are sensible and can add impact to your talk.

Don't be daft enough to use Eilean nan Roan as an example for your talk. I chose it because I'm looking at the island as I write this, and because I know about what happened there. The example you choose will be your own, something which you know about, that interests you and has the potential to grab your audience.

Expression

You must speak clearly and make sure that your audience can actually hear you. The first is sometimes a little harder than the second of these. The talk is not a test of elocution, but the words and sentences must be carefully said.

The style and the tone of your talk have to fit the purpose and the people you're speaking to. The style will be determined by your stance or point of view and will reinforce it. In the example I used above, you can probably figure out that the style would be informative, authoritative and the tone might be one of sympathy, regret or anger, depending on how you view the removal of people from their homes. Your delivery strengthens your talk and produces an impact on the listeners. When planning you can decide what style of speaking and what tone will best fit your own topic and purpose. Once you have decided on style and tone, make sure that you use them all through your talk.

Intonation in your delivery is essential if you are not to sound monotonous and boring. If you really know your subject and are keen to share it with your listeners, it is not likely that you will spoil it by using an inappropriate style or tone. This comes back to your choice of topic and purpose.

Don't forget that you are involved in communication here. Although in an individual presentation the audience doesn't talk to you, people listen and form the other part of this communication. It's a two-way process. You must keep an eye and ear on how they react to what you're saying, and make little adjustments to take account of this. If they like it, you'll know, and you can be even more enthusiastic when the audience is with you. If they look puzzled or bored, then you have to liven up, repeat or explain, ask some rhetorical* questions.

Finally, a word about accent, formality and language. Your accent is not part of the assessment so do not try to alter your accent to one that you think is more appropriate for the occasion. The accent you use is part of you and is as good as an accent from any other part of the country. What matters is that you use correct grammar and syntax in your spoken language. Accents are mostly regional, so if you live in Thurso or Edinburgh or Wigtonshire you will probably speak English with an accent that is different from each of the others, and that accent is fine for your talk.

Scotland has three languages. You will probably give your talk in English (though the *Arrangements* don't actually specify this). English is the official language, but about 80% of Scottish people also speak Scots. This is not a debased form of English, and you may use it in Higher for both talking and writing. It's astonishing how many people equate Scots with some kind of second-rate English, professing not to understand it and believing it to be a slovenly form of speaking best kept for the playground. They admire the speech of the legendary 'ferm-loun* frae Buchan speaking the Doric*' but have problems with urban Glaswegian. Fortunately, things are changing, and I hope that your school recognises the difference and encourages the use of Scots where it is appropriate.

The third language of Scotland, and the oldest of them, is Gaelic. The *Arrangements* have nothing to say about that, and so we had better assume that your talk requirements have to be met in English or Scots.

I have chosen to write THE GUIDE in *informal* mode because it better suits my purpose, which is to give advice and information to you as if I were talking to you. The *Arrangements*, on the other hand, are written *formally* because their purpose is to provide teachers with regulatory requirements for teaching and assessment. Similarly, you must assess whether formal or informal speech best suits your purpose and audience, and use the form that is appropriate, as you judge it. With practice, you will not find it difficult to judge the formality of a situation.

Situations for practice will arise during the course and in your day-to-day life. In class, you will have the benefit of teaching and exposure to all sorts of talk and reading and listening and viewing which will bring you to a point where the advice offered here makes much more sense to you. You should, however, spend time on your own and with others in talk activities and also in studying many sources of learning, including speeches and presentations by others, broadcasts, discussions. You learn about talking from reading and writing as well, remember.

Group discussion

The second option within the unit on oral skills is probably familiar to you from Standard Grade, if you completed that course. In addition, many of the skills, and therefore much of what has been said already about individual presentation, apply also to group discussion so I'm not going to repeat it.

The one crucial addition to the required skills is interaction with other people in a group.

Outcome

The outcome, or what you are required to do to succeed in this unit, is simply put.

> *Participate in group discussion.*

Put like that it doesn't sound too difficult. Participating does not, however, mean just turning up and sitting there. Participation is an activity for all of the members of the group, and there are particular requirements for success. There are also additional skills that are associated with this form of oral communication and which need to be demonstrated. Unlike the situation described for individual presentation, discussion involves interactive skills in both talking and listening, and these are what are being assessed. You don't have a captive audience in a discussion, which means that any one of the group can bite back at any time.

That makes discussion sounds like a combative activity where the group members compete with each other. In fact, it's almost the very opposite. The main purpose of discussion is to co-operate towards achieving either a consensus or a conclusion which satisfies those taking part, even though they might not agree in the end. It's a team activity, even though, of course, you will be individually assessed on how well you have met the criteria.

So the main idea to grasp is that discussion involves interacting with others to achieve a common end. You can be equally unsuccessful by saying too much as by saying too little.

Again, it's not only a matter of how much you say, but also how well you say it. Quality as well as quantity matters.

For the unit assessment the group must have at least four members and there must be no help from anyone else (no friendly teacher jogging memories, for example) and you have to meet all the criteria in one go, as for the individual talk.

Performance criteria
Content

In the context of discussion, your purpose is all-important. In individual presentation *you* choose your own topic and purpose: for discussion, however, the likelihood is that *your teacher* will set both of these for the group. You must make sure that all you say and do is directed to that purpose. When you have some contribution to make, it must be appropriate to the discussion's purpose and it must be intended to take the discussion forward. You should always be able to support with detail or evidence any statement or question that you advance.

Structure

I cannot say much about the structure of the discussion here, because that is a matter for the whole group, and particularly for the chairperson, if there is one. For this reason, structure is not one of the criteria on which you will be judged. The overall success or failure of a discussion can depend on the contribution of others. Don't think that this directly affects your performance in assessment, though. Follow what's said about co-operation, and you'll be successful in any discussion, even if the others aren't.

Nevertheless, it will be to your credit if you bring the group back to the purpose if it is straying away from it, because deviating from the purpose means that the implicit structure is in danger of being lost. If you are chairing the discussion then you do have an obligation to maintain a sensible structure for the whole discussion. You can't plan this in detail, because a discussion is a living, developing thing, but it can be planned in outline. That outline depends on the purpose for the discussion. If the topic happens to be a question, the structure plan would include turning the discussion to a direction that enables the participants to answer the question, after a consideration of the different views likely to be contributed.

Expression

When expressing your contributions, you must be clear in your speech, and you have to make sure that you are heard by all the group, even if you appear to be responding to another single individual's statement or question. Your audience is always the whole group. In discussion you must be able to use body language, so-called non-verbal skills, probably even more than in individual talk.

These skills overlap very much with the skills of talking that we have already covered. Here you are actively interacting with other people, who are listening and talking to the same purpose as you.

You must establish and maintain eye contact with others in the group. This not only tells them that you are speaking to them, but also sends intentional and unintentional signals to them about the message that they are hearing at the same time. Think of what we mean when we say, 'Look me in the eye and say that!' You can convey feelings, such as sincerity, anger, and agreement with a look and a nod. Indeed, you can even do it without the words!

In the same way, you should remember that body alignment and shifts in your position send strong signals to the people you are talking to, as does the use of your hands. This is almost a science in itself. Pay attention to what people do with their bodies and hands when they speak. For practice try observing a discussion, but don't listen to the words. Or better, if you have a video of people talking, turn off the sound and watch. (There's a very good example in the support material issued to teachers for Higher English: your teacher probably has it. It shows a girl talking about body language and demonstrating it, too.) You'll be convinced that body language has a big part to play in conveying our meaning, but a greater part in making clear our feelings and attitude. Look at someone sitting with arms folded while someone talks to them. The message is unmistakable: it is, 'I don't really want to hear this.'

Interacting with the group

Your non-verbal as well as your verbal language must show that you are listening and understanding what others are saying. In other words, you must take a full part in the discussion. You must grasp that trying to talk all the time is counterproductive. If the discussion becomes a monologue you have failed to achieve the purpose of the discussion.

A chairperson sometimes controls turn-taking, but that can lead to a sterile and artificial kind of discussion. There has to be natural turn-taking. You take your opportunity when it's presented, or when you make it. Your turn-taking must include the kind of behaviour that is the marker of discussion: making comments, asking questions, introducing ideas, responding to points already made by others, giving your opinion, challenging opinions offered by others or agreeing with them.

Another area of discussion that is neglected by many is the need to encourage others in the group to speak their views. You must do this, for example, by turning to the person and inviting them to speak with, 'What do you think?'. As well as allowing others to speak and encouraging them to do so, you must acknowledge the status of the chairperson, if there is one, by giving way and responding to invitations and directions when they are presented.

Incidentally, humour helps discussion along. There's no need always to be completely po-faced about a subject. Irony can sit quite well with the most serious of subjects.

Chairing a discussion

Even if there is no designated chairperson, it is a very good strategy – if you feel capable of it – to assume, from time to time, responsibility for keeping the discussion on track.

Remind others of the direction in which you are supposed to be heading, analyse what has been said so far, and summarise the position reached at intervals. You can score valuable assessment points for this kind of contribution, if you can do it and do it well.

There are no specific criteria set down in the *Arrangements* to cover the business of chairing a discussion. It may be helpful, however, to have some advice about this task, since it is quite likely to come up during the course.

The chair should introduce the topic and the purpose of the discussion so that it's clear to everyone in the group what they are to do. As for individual talk, there are better ways of doing this than simply and boldly stating the obvious, especially by announcing it as if you were reading a statement or making an announcement in a railway station. An imaginative way of doing this is certain to improve the quality of the discussion that follows it. A broad comment on the issue for discussion helps enormously. Study the kind of remarks made by a chairman of TV discussions or panels. Be aware, however, that a TV chairperson has a role that is slightly different from yours. The difference is that, as chair, you still have to play a full part in the discussion, as each other member of the group must.

During the discussion, the chair should encourage all members to speak, ask questions and summarise from time to time. At the close, the chair is expected to bring things to a conclusion by indicating what you have discussed and what you have collectively decided. Playing the role of chair does not give your opinions any greater weight than those of others, and it doesn't give you any priorities in turn-taking either. It certainly does not give you the right to sum up with your own views as if they were the conclusion reached by this democratic business of discussion. The main function of the chair is to keep the discussion on the right track. You do this by encouraging, questioning and initiating directions based on what has already been said . . . or, indeed, should have been said.

Discussion requirements can be summed up by saying that the task of a participant in a discussion is:

- to contribute 'readily but not excessively' (in the words of the *Arrangements*)
- to take account of the contributions of others
- to help the discussion in its communal purpose by trying always to maintain a good relationship with the group.

Critical listening

This bit is going to be short as it's not at all clear whether many schools will offer the option in practice. One of its attractions is that the assessment can be done at one go for a whole class group, rather than individually as for individual presentation and discussion. Another is that the skills needed are almost exactly the oral parallel of skills that are being promoted, learned and assessed in close reading.

The word 'critical' comes from a Greek word meaning I judge, pass judgement. So we get the word 'criticise', meaning to weigh up the good and the bad (not simply to complain).

Be aware that, in this option, it is not your practical oral skills that are being assessed. Here you will be demonstrating your interpretation skills. The difference between this and close reading is that instead of written texts, you will be dealing with spoken examples of communication, such as broadcasts and live presentations including dialogues and speeches, reports, discussions and interviews.

So, critical listening concerns writing or talking about oral skills, that is, being engaged passively with these skills. It's not your ability to use oral skills, but your ability to study, understand, analyse and evaluate oral communication skills as used by other people.

It may not have come through so far in all this information about the Oral Communication Unit, but you will be studying, understanding, analysing and evaluating the oral skills of others in the learning process that leads up to making a presentation or taking part in a discussion. This means that you will be faced with examples of these skills in the teaching that takes place in the course, regardless of which of these three options you actually choose (or, as pointed out earlier, is chosen for you).

For information and advice on critical listening skills, therefore, look back to what is said throughout the sections on close reading (Chapter 4) and on the other oral options in this chapter. Just remember to adjust for the change of mode from reading to listening.

CHAPTER EIGHT

THE SPECIALIST STUDY UNIT

The Specialist Study Unit is the most straight-forward of all to describe and explain. You write an essay or produce a video on a topic chosen by you, with advice from your teacher. What you produce is variously called an investigation, a review or an analysis, depending on which option you decide to tackle.

There are three options from which to choose:

- language
- literature
- oral communication.

If you choose the option that is probably the most popular, literature, there is virtually no change from the old Higher.

Your teacher will be broadly familiar with the arrangements for this unit, because it is so similar to the old Higher English. That fact will help *you*.

The specialist study demands *independent study* from *you*.

Any doubt about the authenticity of student work is deeply damaging to the achievements of all other students, including the important one, YOU.

Following the rules

The *Arrangements* for the specialist study have been made very clear and must be followed if you are to be successful in this unit. The rules about how the study is to be produced are very strict. If you don't follow the step-by-step requirements to guarantee that you have produced the work properly, then you will automatically fail in this unit. If you fail for that reason (i.e. not following the procedure) it doesn't mean just a partial re-assessment to raise the standard of your study. It means going back to square one: your work would be completely disqualified. Effectively it means failing Higher English that year. The rules are covered in some detail from page 74.

> So, I want to emphasize the fact that you can fail in this unit by not following the procedure . . . even though your work reaches the standard of attainment required by the performance criteria. Your work would be disqualified.

Similarities with other units

There is a great deal of overlap between the Specialist Study Unit and other parts of the course, namely:

- the folio
- the critical essay(s) in the Literary Studies Unit
- the critical essay in the external examination.

The investigation that you will produce in this unit becomes the third part of the folio.

The overlap with the Literary Studies Unit (Chapter 6) is considerable, because at least one of the pieces of work you produce there must be a critical essay. The specialist study on literature is like a critical essay somewhat extended in length. Even if you choose the Language option for your specialist study, the essay is going to be quite close in structure and concerns to the critical essay. It still involves understanding, analysis, evaluation and expression in relation to a topic chosen by you.

The overlap with the critical essay in the external examination (Chapter 10) is considerable too, since the critical essays in the unit and the exam are almost the same task.

So, there is no need to say much here about the performance criteria, the activities or the skills involved in the work of producing the specialist study. Just turn back to the relevant section of the book (Chapter 6).

If the option you choose is the literary option, then these truths hold. Just look back to the section of THE GUIDE dealing with the Literary Studies Unit (Chapter 6). If you intend to choose the language option, as it happens, not much is different. The detailing of the criteria wording differs, of course, but you can use the wording of the literature option as a model, and you can make the necessary semantic* changes for yourself without too much difficulty. If you decide to choose the oral communication area, then the performance criteria are a little different, but the parallels are not difficult for you to trace, and you can still use the literature review criteria as a broad model.

The main point for your attention is that the rules of procedure are the same for each variant – literature, language or oral communication – so whatever version you choose, make sure that you stick to the rules for producing the work.

The outcome

The outcome is uncomplicated, even if we look at all three options simultaneously:

- Language – investigate critically a chosen aspect of language use.

■ Literature – review critically his or her own choice of text(s).

■ Oral communication – analyse a selected aspect of oral communication.

So, you produce an extended essay if you choose either of the first two options or, for the third option, you produce an analysis, but not in written form. It is produced on video in spoken form.

The oral communication option

I'll say what there is to say about his third option right now. Despite the fact that I am a very keen advocate of oral skills, I am not recommending this as an option. I say this somewhat reluctantly. Be aware that a very great percentage (80%) of our message in an oral communication is delivered by body language. This might lead you to believe that it is an easy option. Don't be fooled.

First of all, dealing with an oral communication is just as difficult as dealing with a written text or an aspect of language. Secondly, delivering a 10 to 15 minute spoken presentation on video is no easy task. Unless you are going to be well supported in teaching and supervision, as well as with good and reliable video facilities, you should not attempt it. If all the necessary input is available to you, if your teacher is placing a strong emphasis on oral aspects, by using, for example, discussion and presentation methods in teaching and learning, and is covering the Oral Communication Unit seriously and enthusiastically, *and* you are very strong in this area, then go for this variant of the specialist study.

Performance criteria and activities

I've already noted that the performance criteria for the written studies, literature and language, are similar. The activities that contribute to the production of the specialist study are embedded in the whole course and its component units and, broadly speaking, are similar to each other, regardless of the choice you make.

For that reason I am going to allow the conditions for the literature variant to stand for all three. You must make the necessary adjustments where the vocabulary is clearly inappropriate.

The performance criteria are almost exactly the same as those for the critical essay, covering the same four features: understanding, analysis, evaluation, and expression. The examiners and your teacher are looking for:

■ secure understanding

■ accurate and detailed analysis

■ evaluation based on firm evidence.

If you care to look back to the section of THE GUIDE dealing with the Literary Studies Unit (Chapter 6), you will find more discussion of the relevant performance criteria.

Remember that these criteria state what is required for a *basic pass* in the unit, and that you are always going to be trying hard to do much better than that.

You have to know now about the rules for producing the specialist study. Let's look at them step by step.

How to produce the Specialist Study

1 Independent study

You have to do most of the work independently, with minimal support from your teacher. I'll point this out each step of the way.

2 Choosing an option

The first step will be to choose which of the three options you intend to tackle. In reality, while I reckon that you'll be able to make a free choice of literature or language in most schools and colleges, it's very likely that the oral communication option will be restricted by various constraints in many centres. It is quite likely that your teacher will not raise it as an option at all, or will indicate that it cannot be offered. Most students will opt for the literature variant. Notice that the choice is yours, but you must listen to your teacher's advice. The specialist study is intended to have a linkage with the units you have studied in the course, so much will depend on what options have been followed in the course offered in your school or college.

3 Choosing a 'text'

A second step is to identify a 'text'. I'm using the word 'text' as shorthand to cover all three options. In each option there is what we could call a 'text'. In the literature option it really is a literary text, whether it's a novel or short story or a poem. In the language option it might indeed be a written piece that is a text. Alternatively, it may not be a written example of language, but a subject that is more general – spoken language usage in Dundee, for example. In the third option, we can use 'text' to mean a particular instance of spoken (recorded or broadcast, for example) language use.

You will consult your teacher for advice about your choice, **but your teacher will not make the choice for you**. Whatever your text, it must be one that you have chosen, **not one that has been set for you by your teacher**.

If the literary option is the one for you, then the text must be different from any you have studied in the course. Indeed, it is one that you choose because it is of interest to you, and has not been taught to you in the course, or earlier in your schooling.

The text must fulfil four criteria:

1   The text must be approved by your teacher.

2 It must have literary merit.

3 It must be accessible to you.

4 It must be different from the text(s) you use in the exam or the Literary Studies Unit.

The first three of these conditions are closely linked to each other. You must consult your teacher about the text you propose to use. This is so that your teacher can give you on-the-spot advice. No one else can give you detailed advice on your specific choice. I can't give that level of advice here in THE GUIDE. The SQA cannot advise you either. You must act on your teacher's advice. That advice will tell you whether the text is of the quality that will enable you to fulfil the demands of the performance criteria when you write about it. In theory, a brilliant student could produce a high-quality review and critical evaluation of a work that looks unpromising on the face of it. It would be possible to write such a piece on an episode of 'The Broons' in *The Sunday Post*, but this would be exceptional. On the other hand, there is nothing to be gained in choosing a complex novel like James Joyce's 'Finnegans Wake' if you don't understand it . . . in other words, if it isn't accessible to you. Your teacher's advice will be based on balancing the challenge of the text against your perceived ability to cope with it. That is why you must take the advice offered.

The fourth point is self-evident. Your choice has to be different from any you used in the Literary Studies Unit, because any you have used there will have been taught in the course and so is automatically excluded. Concerning the exam exclusion, however, you won't know yet which text you will be dealing with in the exam. You do know that the exam will contain (probably but not necessarily) a text that you have studied in the course. So it can't be used in the Specialist Study anyway. Notice, however, that you cannot use any text that has been taught as part of the course, even if you do not use it in the exam later. It's not just the double use of it in exam and review that's the problem: it's the fact that it has to be one that you have studied independently, having chosen it yourself.

Incidentally, don't be tempted to try to get round this rule, hoping that it won't be noticed. There are complicated checking mechanisms for this at SQA, and any duplicate use means that the marks for the second one are cancelled. For most students, losing all the marks for a major part of the assessment package would lead to outright failure in the overall exam. Remember that you gain an overall pass by aggregating (adding up) all the marks you gain in the various components of the assessment system.

4 Choosing a topic

The next step is important if you are to have any real hope of success in your specialist study. In fact, I can tell you that the main cause of failure by students, who could otherwise demonstrate the necessary skills, is that they choose a topic which does not allow them to demonstrate the skills and competencies called for by the performance criteria for the specialist study.

Within the option, within the text, you choose a **topic**. The more focused and concentrated the topic is, the more likely you are to be successful in dealing with it. A topic is not, for example, *Lord of the Flies* – the whole novel is not a suitably focused topic. You might look at 'Good and Evil in *Lord of the Flies*', or better, 'Some Aspects of Symbolism in *Lord of the Flies*'. You might know that William Golding was concerned with good and evil in his writing and that it pervades this work. For that reason, the focus is diffuse. If you chose to deal with some aspects of symbolism in the novel, your focus would be sharper. The Principal Assessor's (Examiner's) Report year after year refers to this important matter and points out that many students fail because their choice of topic is too unfocused and makes it impossible for the student to deal with a wide-ranging coverage within the set limits, or indeed, at all.

5 Deciding on your aim

The next step is to work out an aim for your study and here you should again consult your teacher for advice.

Think of the aim as simply making a statement of what you intend to do in the specialist study. The examiner will measure your success against your stated aim. This is why it is important to make clear at the start what you intend to do, or if you like, to say what your piece of writing is going to be about. To make this as plain as possible, see it like this: for the specialist study, the task is actually set by you, for you to achieve. You choose the text, the topic, and the purpose, and thus set yourself the task. This makes your aim exactly the same as a question in the examination. In the examination, what you write is measured for success against the question. So, since you have the luxury of setting your own question, you should make sure that it's one that you can answer well, and one that will help you to display all the qualities required to pass in the unit. Whatever it is that you intend to achieve by your writing on your topic in the specialist study, make sure that you actually say so near the beginning of your piece.

Controlled conditions

I've mentioned already that there are published rules which apply to all students when producing their specialist studies, and these are a condition of gaining an award.

The conditions are put in place to help authenticate your work as your own. The controlled conditions do not actually include having to sit and write your study in an examination room with an invigilator. Certainly some time will be spent in class in the task of writing, but most of the work on your study will take place outwith school or college, in your own time and place. The class time will be used for teaching you research methods, giving advice in general about writing such a work. It will not be used by your teacher for teaching you directly about the subject of your study. Indeed, your teacher is prohibited from doing that, and his or her intervention is restricted to general comments on your drafts and ideas.

Schedule conditions

Some of the conditions have been discussed above. There are also conditions that are concerned with the actions you must complete against a schedule of deadlines that will be set by your school or college. Note that the dates are set by your school or college and will vary from place to place. The actual items on this schedule are not negotiable, however. You must complete them, and in line with your given deadlines. These will be published and will form a contract between you and the centre. If you fail to meet the schedule, you are in danger of failing in this unit.

You will be given dates when:

- you must present a draft title and proposals for your study
- you must provide an outline plan for your study
- you must submit a first draft of your study
- you must complete a final draft of your study.

Presentation conditions

The second group of conditions relates to the presentation of your work:

- The study must be within the prescribed range in length.
- The range at Higher is 1200–1800 words including quotations.
- At Intermediate 2 it is 800–1800 words.

There are penalties for falling outwith the range, but particularly for exceeding the limit. It's amazing how many studies, especially the very long ones, are described as being 1798 words in length. Sometimes they are so obviously over-length that a simple glance at them is enough to alert the marker to the fact. Markers actually do count the words, and refer overlength studies to the Principal Examiner to be penalised. It isn't worth exceeding the length requirement: don't do it. Excessive length can lose you up to 25% of the marks available. That penalty is designed to lead to failure, since few students' performances would recover.

There are several other conditions also:

- The work must be your own. If there is any suggestion of personation (somebody else doing it for you) it will be rejected by your teacher and by SQA, if it even gets that far.
- You should acknowledge your sources by listing any secondary texts (i.e. other books) you have consulted.
- **Do not plagiarise**. If you plagiarise (i.e. use the unacknowledged words and/or ideas of another person and deliberately represent them as your own) your work will be disqualified and rejected by your teacher. If the examiners discover such work, it

will lead to the cancellation of your award in English, and quite possibly to the cancellation of your whole certificate . . . that is, in all your subjects.

The message to students in this part of the course is clear. If you intend to employ the services of a tutor, make very sure that you have one who understands very clearly that this is an area of the course where a tutor has very limited opportunities for intervention. Excessive support is prohibited, and could cause you to have your work disqualified. If you have a tutor, show him or her this paragraph.

Writing your study

This section of THE GUIDE provides information and advice about the specialist study. It doesn't attempt to teach you how to write it. That will be happening during the course: in this unit itself, in the Literary Studies Unit, in the Language Studies Unit and also in the Oral Communication Unit. It is a part of the course that should bring you some pride in your work. You'll be writing about a choice of subject that interests you, and where you can communicate your own original ideas.

Don't be too worried about the somewhat pretentious title for this unit. The 'specialist' part means no more than the fact that you will specialise for this unit of the course in literature or language or oral communication. You should, however, in the course of your research in preparation for writing your study, learn a great deal about your chosen topic, and you will become a kind of expert on it. That gives most people a feeling of satisfaction.

CHAPTER NINE

THE PERSONAL STUDIES FOLIO

There is an unavoidable sense of déjà vu* in this short section on the folio. You already know from reading Chapter 1 of THE GUIDE that the folio contents are simply coursework you have done in the various units – the Language Unit, the Oral Communication Unit and the Specialist Studies Unit. 'Products generated for assessment purposes in certain areas may also be used for external assessment', as the *Arrangements* put it.

The work is done in class, put into the folio and sent off to Dalkeith for external assessment. Though the folio has already been assessed internally, that assessment was used to see that the work reached the minimum standard for passing in the various units. External assessment is for grading purposes. The unit assessment measured up to grade C only: the examiners measure them for further merit, at grade B or A. The external assessment on the folio content is worth 40% of the overall course award for your Higher English. So it's essential that your folio be submitted in good order.

Remember that your folio contains three items:

1   Writing from Unit 1

2   A pass in the Oral/aural Communication Unit

3   Your specialist study.

We have already looked at the detailed requirements of each of these three pieces of work in the relevant chapters. Since the Oral Communication Unit is internally assessed, the external examiners do nothing further with it, other than note your score for aggregation into your overall mark.

As you know, the other two items are real physical pieces of writing (or videotape if you've opted for the oral variant in your specialist study).

You are responsible for producing the work in your folio under the conditions already set out earlier in the sections of THE GUIDE covering the Language Studies Unit, the Specialist Studies Unit and the Literary Studies Unit. Your teacher is responsible for ensuring that the folio is assembled and dispatched to Dalkeith in good time, but can do that only if you have completed the work and handed it in in time and under the conditions that apply. This means normally that you have to have passed in each of the units by completing the work and meeting the criteria.

Exceptionally, it is possible for your teacher to submit a mark for your work if, at the time for sending in the folio, you have not achieved a pass in a unit. Your incomplete mark can go forward to contribute to your overall mark for the course. You will not be awarded a certificate (in plain speech, you won't have passed your Higher English), however, until you have managed to pass the failed unit as well. This is not a route that you should attempt to follow.

If you have failed a unit, there are special circumstances in which you can actually get the overall award. This means having to do brilliantly in the exam, thus overturning the need to have passed the units. Don't depend on this arrangement, because achieving it is always going to be very, very exceptional.

Make sure that you have achieved a pass in all the units before the folio is sent in. Passing the units indicates that you have a fair chance of passing the external exam and that it is worth your while sitting it. Not having passed one or more units at this stage indicates that, in your teacher's estimate, you are not likely to pass the exam.

The folio is submitted in a special folder provided by SQA. Your teacher will have received your pieces of work from you (possibly at different times during the course, for storing). Inside the folio cover there is a statement that you have to sign and date, and one that your teacher completes. These require you and your teacher to certify that the work is your own and that it has been completed under the proper conditions. In the absence of these signed statements, enquiries result.

You must:

1   complete and submit a piece of writing from Unit 1

2   have passed the Oral/aural Communication Unit

3   complete and submit your Specialist Study.

The piece of writing is detailed in the Language Studies Unit (Chapter 5).

The oral component of the folio is detailed in Chapter 7.

The specialist study and its conditions are described in detail in Chapter 8.

It might be encouraging to be reminded that the folio is worth 40% of the whole total of marks for the Higher – 12.5%, 12.5% and 15% for the items in the order they appear at the start of this section.

CHAPTER TEN

THE EXAMINATION: PAPER I AND PAPER II

Examination strategies

We've come to the examination time, when you actually sit your Higher English – that sunny day in May when you would much rather be outside, or anywhere else for that matter.

Let me remind you that the exam is worth 60% of your award and the other 40% is already determined by your assessment for the units and the folio. By the time of the exam, the units have been completed and your folio is in the hands of the examiners.

The examination requirements have already been mentioned much earlier in THE GUIDE, but only in outline (Chapter 1). The work that is involved in the examination has been the subject of your learning and the teaching throughout the course, and this is where you apply your knowledge and skills to show that you can meet the standards needed to earn your certificate. The course is not there to teach you to sit the exam. The exam can only *sample* some of what you have learned over the course. So what you put into the exam is no more than a fraction of what you have acquired in your education.

As we have seen, English is not simply a collection of facts and information, unlike many other subjects that are what we call 'content-based'. This has a bearing on what the exam is like, and also on the vexed question of 'revision'. There are some words of wisdom about studying and revision still to come (Chapter 12).

I hope that you can see that your education is what you bring to the exam, and so you should be able to face it with a lot of confidence. The examiners can only invite you to show some of what you can do, and you should have much more to spare.

Some of the work you will do in the examination has also been discussed earlier, because the exam is sampling some of the work done for internal assessment. There is nothing in the exam that you have not faced before in the course. If we look again at what you have to attempt in the exam, you'll see that it's nothing to be feared.

You have the benefit of open-book conditions in the **internal** assessment of critical essays, and this is a wonderful help in coping with the pressure. Open-book conditions are also available in Advanced Higher, but **not** in Higher external exams.

Preparing to sit the exam

I start with the obvious:

1   Make sure that you get hold of your personal copy of the exam timetable supplied to your school/college by SQA for you.

2   Highlight all your exams on the timetable and keep it where you see it every day. If you're attending school or college, it's quite possible that you will be off on 'study leave'. This means that you don't have people around to remind you to turn up! Every year, students turn up on the wrong day, and while that's okay if you turn up on a day before the exam, it is *not* okay if you turn up later. The only thing to be done then is to wait till the next round of exams.

3   Don't stay up late the night before, especially not doing last-minute studying. Get a good night's sleep.

4   Check the exam timetable carefully and make sure that you have the correct time as well as the correct date. Arrive at the exam room well before the start time.

5   Bring two pens, one as a spare. They must have black or blue ink. That's because the markers use red, and the examiners use green.

6   Bring a watch or clock. There might not be one in the exam room, although there should be.

7   Don't bring anything else into the exam room, even blank paper. It's not permitted.

8   When you go to your seat, sit calmly and think relaxing thoughts.

9   When the exam paper and the answer book are given out, the Invigilator will tell you when to fill in your details on the answer book, and then he or she will tell you when to start answering.

The examination papers

This section looks at what the examination consists of. There are variants for Higher and Intermediate (Intermediate requirements follow in brackets).

There are two papers:

Paper I – Close reading
>   2 passages
>   1 hour 30 minutes
>
>
>   (1 passage and 1 hour at Intermediate 2)

Paper II – Textual Analysis and critical essay
>   1 hour 30 minutes

So you can see that the pain will all be over in 3 hours!

Success in exams has got a lot to do with how confident you feel at the exam time. The one main thing that will make you more confident is knowing in advance what you will be facing.

Paper I – Close reading

We have already spent time discussing the kind of texts and questioning you should expect when your close reading skills are being tested. Paper I tests the same skills as the Language Studies Unit (Chapter 4).

The instructions and rubric*

The instructions are written on the front cover of the paper, and SQA uses **bold type** and sometimes BLOCK CAPITALS to draw your attention to them. Ironically, many people don't read them at all!

Make sure that you do, because the format of the paper is not always exactly what you may expect. The design blueprint used by the examiners allows them to make minor changes from time to time. It's not to say that the examiners are sneaky, but it's quite normal for some parts of the exam paper to stay in a particular form for several years, so that people lose sight of the fact that this is only one *possible* form. Then when the examiners decide to change some aspect of the exam, many students and teachers are thrown by it. A few years ago in the old Higher, there was consternation when the practical criticism text appeared as prose after several years of poetry. It was misread by some candidates as a second interpretation passage and led to consequential problems for them in options later in the paper.

Your approach to the exam should be to expect the unexpected every time. Never be surprised!

By the time you come to sit the exam, you'll probably have seen NABS, past papers and specimen papers like the one printed in THE GUIDE (Chapter 11). But it's still possible for new variations to appear in the paper that really matters to you – the one *you* sit.

So, be very wary and read the instructions very carefully, even if it's only to make sure that you have the correct level of Paper in front of you.

The rubric tells you what you have to do to answer the question and, if you do something else, then you create great difficulties for yourself. Question papers are drafted, pulled apart, checked, pre-tested (in another English-speaking part of the world), moderated, proof-read, re-checked and finalised with great care. By the time they get into your hands you can be sure that they are more than precise, so all the words mean what the words say. They will not be ambiguous.

They will simply ask you to read the passages and answer the questions. Notice that you are expected to answer the questions that are printed in the paper, not the ones you wish had been set.

What to do next

First read the passages at normal reading pace. **Do not panic**.

The text

As you read, note the key ideas. The passages will be linked by a common theme or topic. They will be prose, almost certainly, drawn from writing of the kind that you have already studied in the Language Studies Unit. The ideas will be complex and you will have to keep your wits about you. But remember, the exam is not designed to trap you or make you feel inadequate. If you and your teacher have made all the choices of course and units correctly, the exam is something that you can cope with quite adequately. After all, you have been presented for the exam at a level where there is a fair expectation of you passing. You will probably have already achieved a pass in your folio at this level. You are *not* expected to fail.

The questions

Next, read the questions and, as you do so, make mental notes of those you reckon you can answer, or for which you can find the part of the passage that holds the answer. The questioning will be sequential for the most part, i.e. it will trace the progress of the text from the start through to the end. There will, however, be questions that refer to the text(s) as a whole.

Never even dream of starting with the questions and attempting to answer them by picking up areas of the text where you think there is a glimmer of connection with the question. That leads to disaster.

When you have seen the questions and noted the gaps in your information or understanding, read the passages again. At this stage you will have an idea of the passages and a fair idea of the questions that you think you can answer, or at least you will know where to look for the answers.

This time, as you read, you are operating in reverse. This time you are checking the text for reference to the questions you have not yet 'cracked', and at the same time are confirming areas of questioning you feel that you have in control.

You will be surprised by the level of understanding you can reach on the second reading. Things you missed the first time jump into place. Ideas unfold and become clear, nuances of meaning and tone leap out at you. Now you are ready to answer the questions.

You can pick up your pen . . . again if you've already used it for note-making. The question paper is yours to retain if you wish, so there's no harm in using it for note-making. You can use your answer book for note-making, too, if it helps. You will not have any spare paper for notes, because you are not allowed to take any into the exam room. If you make notes on your answer paper remember to cancel them before you hand in your answer paper at the end of the exam.

From your previous work in the Language Studies Unit, you will know that to answer close reading questions you have to:

- show your *understanding*

- present your *analysis*

- offer your *evaluation*.

These have all been explained in Chapter 4.

The different types of questions will not be arranged in neat groups under these headings when you actually sit the exam. So you have to be able to recognise each type of question when you see it, because this determines the form of your answer. Recognising the question type is easy, however. The questions will have a coded reference letter beside them (U, A or E) to indicate to you which of the three aspects they are concerned with: understanding, analysis or evaluation. When you attempt the questions, you must make sure that your answer-type fits the question-type.

The main thing, you will remember, is not to approach all questions as if they are about meaning. You should get hold of old examination papers for interpretation (they don't have to be 'Higher Still' versions of the past papers: the old Higher papers up till at least 2001 will do well). Study the questioning carefully and note which question-types are which. Some (past) question papers have the three types of question set out in headed sections to identify their purposes. Other past question papers use the U, A, E coding system. What you have to do is observe the typical wording of these question-types, and transfer these recognition signals to the kind of question paper you will sit. In this way, you will begin to understand very well what is expected in your answers.

Identifying question-types is not a complex matter. There is a limit to the ways in which questions can be asked, and it becomes clear when you read them routinely which particular kind of response they are looking for. You should be looking for interrogatory word-signals such as How? Why? What? What effect? Formulate your answers accordingly.

Some 'questions', of course, aren't really questions. They are instructions. Word-signals to look out for are Show. . . Quote. . . Compare. . . Explain. . .

In the box opposite is list of vocabulary that you are expected to know and be able to use when you are working on close reading question papers particularly, but also generally as part of your learning. The examiners will use them in the questions, so you will need to know their meanings and use. This list is not exhaustive* but it is comprehensive.

Words that you should know:

Adjective	Effective	Refer to the text
An expression	Ending	References
Anecdote	Evaluate	Reinforce
Appropriate	Evidence	Revealed
Argument (of the passage)	Explain the function of	Setting
By referring to	Factors	Show
By close reference to the text	Highlights (something)	Show how
	Identify	Sound
Climax	Illustrated	Stance
Comment	Image	Structure
Comment on	Imagery (usually metaphor, simile or personification)	Stylistic feature
Compare		Substantiate
Confirm	Immediate context	Summarise
Context	Inverted commas	Synonym
Contrast	Justify	The use of examples or illustration
Conveyed	Link	
Deduce	Mood	To what extent
Delivering (information)	Negative	Tone
Develops	Perceived purpose	Word choice
Differentiate	Phrases	Word order
Distinguish (between)	Punctuation	Writer's purpose
Drawn from	Quotation	Writer's standpoint

Writing your answers

Take note of the mark allocation alongside each question. This gives a clue to the kind of answer expected. A single mark almost always means that the question is straightforward and that no more than one piece of information is being called for. Questions asking you to quote, for example, are frequently of this type.

Higher mark allocations indicate that the question is more complex. Often this means that there is an (unintentionally) half-hidden additional part to the question. The question might ask you to *support* your answer: it might demand *more than one piece of information* in the answer; it might mean that the question calls for an *extended* answer.

You are expected to write in sentences for many answers, but not for all. Do not waste time writing out the question or even incorporating its format into your answer. Do not write sentences when you are just asked to quote from the text. People worry about this, but the absolutely definitive position is that the *quotation alone* is required – there is no deduction of marks for simply writing down the right quotation. That, after all, is what the question asks you to do.

> A particularly badly-managed type of question asks you to say what you think about some aspect of the writer's ideas, or tone, or style. It also requires you to answer 'with detailed reference to the text' in order to support your answer.
>
> As well as giving your opinion, you must back up your answer by either quoting the exact words or describing the part of the passage that you believe demonstrates the point the writer is making. You must then justify your answer by showing the link between your ideas and the writer's words. This is as much an important part of the expected answer as your opinion. Often, in fact, more marks are given for the support than for the claim you are making. Indeed, sometimes the question actually gives you the idea and simply asks you to provide the support for it by quoting or describing the author's words.

Using your own words

Some questions ask you to write in your own words. Generally speaking that is what you should do for most questions (except where you are asked for quotations). So, if they ask for your own words, that's what you must give. If you simply lift words from the text, you get nil for that answer.

Lifting words from the text is like saying to the examiner,

> *'I don't know the answer exactly, but I know that it has something to do with this part of the text, so maybe you would be good enough to extract the precise bit for me, translate it into your words and pretend that I wrote it?*

The examiners would really like to help you, but this is something they don't do for you.

You would be as well to write nothing at all for that answer, because the credit you can gain for it is the same either way. None.

Identifying your answers

You should take care to identify your answers in the same code as the questions. This is helpful to the examiners, but more importantly, it's helpful to you. It also allows you to be sure that you have answered all the required questions. This is especially important if you have to answer questions in a different order from that in which they appear in the paper. You ask 'Am I allowed to do that?'; the answer is 'Yes, of course you are.' Normally, writing these out-of-sequence answers at the end of your other answers is the best ploy. It's also possible to leave a space with the question number beside it, so that you know when you are checking your work that you have to come back to it. You should always try to provide some kind of answer, even if it's only partial. Markers will give credit for what you provide, but they can't give you marks if there's absolutely nothing there at all.

Handwriting

Write so that the marker can read what you have written. It would be a great pity if your brilliant answers were indecipherable because, if the marker genuinely can't read what you have written, you won't get any marks.

Don't misunderstand this point. The markers are all very carefully instructed in the art of *positive marking*. They do not proceed by looking for what you do wrong: they look always for where they can give you credit, and will always try to read your scrawl, if that's what you hand in. Their charity has limits, however. Ill-mannered scribbling and marker patience don't go well together.

Timing

Exams are timed to give the same conditions for all candidates.

You have 90 minutes to read the texts, read the questions, answer the questions, think, check and redraft. There are two texts: there are three sets of questions, one on each text and one set of (usually) comparative questions covering the two together.

- Allow time for reading the texts twice.
- Allow time for scanning the questions and making notes.
- Allow time for writing your answers.
- Allow time for checking your work.

Not everyone works at the same pace, but the time allocation is designed to be fair, so that all should have time to finish. The exam has been pre-tested and the examiners know whether it is fair in timing for candidates.

You should think about spending half the available time on each text and set of questions, reserving say 5 or 10 minutes for checking. That leaves a good 40 minutes for each text and questions. One text might be longer than the other, and the questions on both texts might require slightly extended answers. So, although it makes some sense to halve the time between texts, you have to be flexible on the day.

Keep an eye on the clock during the exam and pace yourself accordingly. The exam room is supposed to have a clock that is visible to all candidates, but take a watch and put it on the desk where you can see it.

If you spend a shorter time on one text it won't matter. But if you spend a very long time on the first, for example, you will run into difficulties. If you are stuck on a question and find time passing, move on and come back to it later, especially if it's a low-value question (with few marks allocated). The answers often come more readily the second time round. If you do this, however, don't forget to come back to it! Make large and obvious marks beside the question on the paper and also mark where you have left space for it in the answer book. Make sure that you attempt all the high-value questions since that way you will attract some credit even if you don't gain all the marks.

If you know what to expect in the exam you will be confident in your ability to cope with the exam timing. The essential thing is to move forward at a steady pace and in full awareness of what time there is still available. Time will pass quickly, as I'm sure you know, but if you are in control of your progress, there will certainly be enough of it.

Checking your work

The important final thing you must do before you hand in your answer book to the invigilator is to check your work and the question paper. Don't try to do this as the invigilator is taking the answer book away from you because by then the examination is over. You should leave a good few minutes at the end to carry out a check and redraft anything that is not quite right. It really pays off. The parts that you can improve will surprise you. In the white heat of the exam you leave out words, you leave out parts of questions, you write things twice, you mis-spell words that you know perfectly well. You omit punctuation. Putting these flaws right could make the difference between a pass and a fail.

This part of the examination is not assessing your writing skills, because it is concerned with reading skills, but you should still present your answers in the way you would like the marker to read them, especially if your wee mistakes begin to impede communication. The marker can give you credit only for what is there to be read.

Paper II – Textual analysis and critical essay

You will see that Paper II has two parts: both of these will be familiar to you because you have met them before in the Literary Studies Unit. Both parts concern literature and test your literary skills, but by two different means.

Part I – Textual analysis

The first part deals with textual analysis – it used to be called practical criticism. As you can see if you have a look now at the specimen question paper (Chapter 11), there is a passage or extract and questions for you to answer. It looks like interpretation all over again, but there *are* differences.

We are dealing with the same skills that were tested in the Literary Studies Unit: your ability to analyse and evaluate imaginative literature. Paper II as a whole is concerned with literary criticism. This first part presents you with an unseen piece of imaginative writing and invites you to demonstrate your skills on it. The second part of the paper offers you the chance to demonstrate these skills in a different way – by writing an essay about some text that you have already studied in depth. So, although it requires the same skills, these are demonstrated against a text whose ideas are already well known to you.

The text

The text will be a piece of imaginative literature rather than the non-fiction of the close reading passages in Paper I. There is a tendency for the text to be poetry, but no guarantee that it will be!

The questions

The questions on the text fall into two groups:

- analysis

- appreciation.

If you look now at the specimen paper, you will see that about two-thirds of the marks are for analysis and about one-third is for appreciation. These values are not set in tablets of stone, however, and the paper that you sit may vary a little from this format. The main thing to note is that there will be few, if any, questions with low-mark values.

Writing your answers

Here we are not concerned only with literal meaning of words, for example. Each of the questions requires an *extended* answer, and many of them will have more than one part, so there are actually more tasks than are identified by question numbers or letters. You must make sure that you do not omit any of the parts in your answers. Pay close attention to the fact that the 'supporting' part of the questions is worth as much or more than the initial task in the question.

Use the marks allocation to form an idea of the kind of answer expected. The number of marks tells you roughly what to aim for in terms of length, number of points, and depth of explanation.

It's usually best to be comprehensive in your explanations, but keep an eye on your timing.

In the analysis section, the question-setters frequently ask you to answer in relation to specified lines or parts of the text. Answers which actually depend on lines or parts of the text other than these gain no marks, so be wary of this.

The appreciation questions call for a short essay. You can see this from the marks allocation. Read the rubric very carefully and note any special instruction that follows it, for this is telling you the structure and purpose of your writing. It is essential to back up your ideas by quoting or referring directly to the words and ideas used by the writer of the text. You are trying here to show your understanding and appreciation of the text, and your writing ought to make clear your personal stance and opinion of what you have read, but you must be able to show that your ideas can be supported by the way the writer has conveyed his or her thoughts to you. While there are no right and wrong answers in this area, whatever you think has to be justified reasonably from the text.

Timing

For Part 1, the examiners will normally give you an idea of the time you should spend on it. The passage will usually be quite short, and the questions few in number. Do not be deceived by this. Writing extended answers will take all the time available if you are making a proper job of it.

Using your own words

You'll find that the questions don't explicitly tell you to use your own words. You will realise that this does not apply quite so obviously, mainly because we are not so much dealing with the meaning of words and phrases to be interpreted as we were in the close reading.

Identifying answers, handwriting, timing and checking

The advice I gave in the close reading section on these matters (pages 84–86) applies in exactly the same way here, and you should look back to that advice and follow it.

Part 2 – Critical essay

In this part of the examination, you are again facing something that you have experienced before. You will be familiar with what you have to do from your work in the units and folio. Here we can concentrate on those aspects of the task that are in any way different from those previous situations. The differences arise simply from the fact that you will be working under external exam conditions. There will be:

1   limited time allocation

2   no access to texts

3   no access to reference works

4   no consultation

5   a task which is pre-determined by others.

These set the exam conditions apart from the relatively 'real-world' conditions that surround the writing of your specialist study or coursework tasks that you have enjoyed (?) during the course.

Choosing the text

Part 2 of this paper is an invitation to write an essay on a literary text that you choose from those you have studied in the course. Actually, it could be a text that you have read privately and have studied on your own account, but you can reflect on the wisdom of such a choice.

You will have studied a number of texts in different genres during the course. If you have worked well and the course has been liberal, you will have a choice of several texts to call upon in each genre. You will choose only *one* of these to write about here, remember. Some candidates cheerfully write several essays on a group of texts despite the fact that the instructions printed in the paper remind them in BLOCK LETTERS to choose only ONE.

Note that your choice excludes writing about any text you wrote about in your specialist study. And your specialist study must be based on a text that you have not used in the Literary Studies Unit. There is a checking system to make sure that anyone who uses the same text twice gets no marks at all for this part of the exam.

Tackling the critical essay

You will probably have a fair idea before you enter the exam room of what you intend to write about, but treat this pre-determined idea with caution. First of all, read over the choices on offer in each of the four sections – drama, prose, poetry and mass media. Only if you arrive at the exam having studied one single possible text are the options truly limited. If you are in that position, your course hasn't been adequate.

While you might well know all there is to know about a certain text, the thing that really matters is the rubric – the form of the question. In the exam you must answer the *exact question* that is printed in front of you. There is always the possibility that the question will not be suitable for the text you have in mind. You must read the question and decide how well your preferred text can be used to meet the demands of the question, not the other way round. You should weigh up which question and which text from your reading are best matched to allow you to demonstrate your skill and knowledge.

Essentially, whichever question you choose, your approach is the same. You use your knowledge and understanding of the text to address the particular slant of the question. Choose wisely.

Advice on using a mass media text

If your course has included study of the mass media as a prominent part, then the matter of choosing and writing your essay is the same as for the other genres. If, however, you have not made any particular and detailed study of the media, do not even dream of attempting to answer a question from this section. Any such attempt is doomed to outright failure. The study of the media has to be as thorough as for any other genre, and if you have not undertaken such study, you are not equipped to tackle it.

Taking account of the questions

When scanning the questions you will notice that they have individual built-in limitations that affect your choice of text and your ability to answer the question.

Pay careful attention to such qualifications as these, taken at random from question papers:

- in which a character's personality changes
- in which symbolism plays an important part

- in which loyalty . . . proves decisive

- whose setting contributes significantly

- involves an unpleasant truth

- in both style and content

- a love poem

- a dramatic monologue

- whose opening scenes

- a tragic hero or heroine

- towards the end.

All of these are conditions or constraints that influence the choice of text. The text you choose *must* have the required features, and you must be able to demonstrate that it does in your answer. So, writing about the last act of Hamlet if the question asks for discussion of the opening scene is not an option; writing about Wilfred Owen's *Dulce et Decorum Est* as if it were a love poem would also raise some difficulties. In saying this, the markers are obliged to accept the candidate's interpretation of the rubric if there is any way at all in which it can be justified, so long as the candidate proves their case.

It goes without saying that writing about a text of a genre different from that required by the question is liable to serious penalties. An example would be writing about a poem when choosing a question from the drama section. People do it, regularly, and suffer the consequences.

Planning your answer

It is sensible to plan what you want to say in line with the question and with the features of the text in mind. Make a brief written plan, think about it, and then stick to it. Your plan can be noted in the answer book and should be cancelled (crossed through) before you hand in your work. Without a plan, you will waste valuable time trying to restructure your essay part way through, or wondering what to say next once you have started. You have only 45 minutes to complete the whole task, so there is no time to waste.

Writing your answer

Make sure that you state clearly what your aim is, then carry it out and conclude by indicating that you have done what you set out to do. Your aim is determined by the rubric. It is good practice to draw attention, in each of the various points that you make, to the fact that you are supporting the general line of your argument.

You must avoid the prepared essay approach. Churning out a standard essay means that you ignore the specific requirements of the rubric for the question being addressed on the day of the exam. It's a dead give-away.

Your essay should show the examiners that you are aware of what is needed. The points they are looking for are:

- attention to the rubric

- knowledge of the text

- personal stance

- critical awareness.

In plain language, your essay should tell the examiner that you are answering the question relevantly, that you know and understand the text you are writing about, that you have the ability to make clear your own personal opinions of the text (examiners really do want to hear your views, not just an echo of your teacher's words) and that you have learned something about the language and methods of literary criticism.

Identifying answers, handwriting, timing and checking

What has been said already in connection with Paper 1 under these headings (pages 84–86) applies equally to the business of writing the critical essay, and you should look back to those sections now.

Language competence

There is one final consideration to be added here. The critical essay should be written in continuous formal prose and should meet the standards of written competence required for Higher English. You must write in sentences and paragraphs. Your spelling is expected to be accurate, and the writing should be stylish rather than mundane or mediocre. Particularly avoid the comma-splice. IT IS FATAL. It is the one feature of an answer that can single-handedly result in failure, regardless of the quality of the answer otherwise.

When you have handed in your Paper II answer book, you can go home and study for the subjects that follow English in the exam timetable. Then you can look forward to the day in August when there is a scene like the one on page 15. It's Davie the Postman handing you your fully deserved certificate.

Work paid off!

CHAPTER 11

SPECIMEN PAPERS

Time: 1 hour 30 minutes

Paper I: Specimen Question Paper

You should attempt all questions.

The total value of the Paper is 60 marks.

Interpretation

There are TWO passages and questions.

Read the passages carefully and then answer all the questions which follow. **Use your own words whenever possible and particularly when you are instructed to do so.**

You should read it to:

> understand what the author is saying about childhood experience and its influence on him as a writer (**Understanding—U**);

> analyse his choice of language, imagery and structures to recognise how they convey his point of view and contribute to the impact of the passage (**Analysis—A**);

> evaluate how effectively he has achieved his purpose (**Evaluation—E**).

A code letter, (U, A, E) is used alongside each question to give some indication of the skills being assessed. The number of marks attached to each question will give some indication of the length and kind of answer required.

Passage 1

In the passage below, William McIlvanney, author of the novel "Docherty", remembers his upbringing and considers its significance in his development as a writer.

> I remember as a boy being alone in the living-room of our council-house in Kilmarnock. I would be maybe 11 years old. I was lying in front of the coal fire with my head resting on an armchair. It was, I think, late on a winter afternoon. The window had gone black and I hadn't put the light on, enjoying the small cave of brightness and heat the fire had hewn
5 from the dark. Perhaps I was a far traveller resting by his camp-fire. Perhaps I was a

knight keeping vigil for the dawn when wondrous deeds would be done. For I could be many people at that time as I still can.

I don't know how I came to be alone at that time in that place. In our house with six not unnoticeable presences, it wasn't an easy trick to be alone, even without counting the cavalcade of aunties and uncles and cousins and friends who seemed to be constantly passing through. I wonder if I had come home from school to find the house empty. But that seems improbable. My mother was a ferocious carer who had an almost mystical capacity to conjure solid worries out of air that to the rest of us looked untroubled and clear. Maybe somebody else was supposed to be with me and had gone out briefly.

I don't know. I am simply aware of myself there. The moment sits separate and vivid in my memory, without explanation, like a rootless flower. Whoever I was being, traveller or knight, I must have been tired. For I fell asleep.

The awakening was strange. I think I must have been aware of the noise of people entering the house, one of those slow fuses of sound that sputteringly traverses the unconscious until it ignites into waking. My consciousness and the room came into the light together. My eyes were bruised with brightness. What I saw seems in retrospect to have had the shiningness of newly minted coins, all stamped unmistakably as genuine, pure metal, the undepreciable currency of my life.

What I saw in fact was pretty banal. My father had his hand on the light-switch he had just pressed. My mother was beside him. They were both laughing at what must have been my startled eyes and my wonderment at being where I was. Around them was a room made instantly out of the dark. It was a very ordinary room. But it was wonderful. How strange the biscuit barrel was where my mother kept the rent-money. How unimaginable was the image of Robert Burns with the mouse, painted on glass by my uncle. How incorrigibly itself the battered sideboard became. The room was full of amazing objects. They might as well have come from Pompeii.

And at the centre of them were two marvellously familiar strangers. I saw them not just as my mother and father. I knew suddenly how dark my father was, how physical his presence. His laughter filled the room, coming from a place that was his alone. My mother looked strangely young, coming in fresh-faced from the cold and darkness, her irises swallowing her pupils as she laughed in the shocking brightness. I felt an inordinate love for them. I experienced the transformation of the ordinary into something powerfully mysterious.

I'm convinced that that moment in the living-room at St Maurs Crescent is one of the experiences from which *Docherty* (and perhaps everything I've written) grew. It was a moment which has had many relatives. When I consider them, I realise that they have several features in common.

One of them is a belief in the grandeur of the everyday, where the ordinary is just the unique in hiding. As it says in *Docherty*, "messiahs are born in stables". That being so, as a boy I kept finding Bethlehem round every corner. So many things amazed me.

There were the stories surrounding me, for a start. *Docherty*, I should think, began its gestation in the mouths of the people all around me. Our house was an incredible talking-shop. As the youngest of four, I seem to have grown up with an intense

50 conversation going on endlessly about me as my natural habitat. By one of those casually important accidents of childhood, the youngest of us had to sleep in a fold-down bed in the living-room. Lack of space had its advantages. This meant that from a very early age, I could be involved, however marginally, in these debates, often going to sleep with the sound of disputation as a lullaby.

55 To this continuing seminar on life and the strange nature of it came many visiting speakers. Our house often felt to me like a throughway for talk. Relatives and friends were always dropping in. They brought news of local doings, bizarre attitudes, memorable remarks made under pressure, anecdotes of wild behaviour. Most of it was delivered and received with a calmness that astonished me. I vaguely sensed, early on, the richness they were casually living among, rather as if a traveller should come upon
60 the Incas using pure gold as kitchen utensils. The substance that would be *Docherty* was beginning to glint for me in fragments of talk and caught glimpses of living.

Cognate to my awareness of the rich and largely uncommemorated life around me was a fascination with language. Given my background, I was lucky to be in a house where books were part of the practical furniture, not there as ornaments but to be read and
65 talked about. My mother was the source of the activity. My sister and my two brothers had established reading as a family tradition by the time I was old enough to join in. Only my father, someone—it has always seemed to me—educated spectacularly below his abilities, was never to be comfortable with books. His presence on the edges of our immersion in reading became, I think, in some way formative for me. I wanted him
70 somehow to be included in the words.

Love of reading led naturally, it seemed at the time, to efforts at writing. If books were not the most sought-after domestic adjuncts in our housing scheme (depraved orgies of poetry-reading behind closed curtains), the desire to actually write poetry could have been construed as proof of mental aberration. But this was my next move, one I effected
75 without being ostracised by my peers because, perhaps, I was also very good at football. Having successfully undergone my masculine rites of passage in the West of Scotland, I could indulge in a little limp-wristed scribbling.

Here again the family situation helped. No one—least of all my father (despite being uninterested in books) —ever questioned the validity of the time I spent arranging
80 words on pieces of paper. I took such tolerance for granted. It was only much later I realised how different it might have been for a working-class boy with ambitions to write. A woman writer-friend told me some years ago of a man she knew who came from a background similar to my own. He was bedevilled by a longing to write plays, much to the embarrassment of his relatives. On one occasion an older brother beat him up
85 severely in an attempt to bring him to his senses and to get him to stop inflicting shame upon the family. Such an attitude had been unimaginable to me in my boyhood.

Passage 2

In this passage, writer and actor Alan Bennett reflects on the ways in which books and parents influenced his childhood and career.

You should read it to:

> understand Alan Bennett's view of the relationship between the world of books and real life (**Understanding—U**);
>
> analyse how he has conveyed this point of view, using humour and tone (**Analysis—A**);
>
> evaluate the effectiveness of the passage by comparison with the previous one by McIlvanney (**Evaluation—E**).

"What you want to be," Mam said to my brother and me, "is gentleman farmers. They earn up to £10 a week." This was in Leeds some time in the early years of the war, when my father, a butcher at Armley Lodge Road Co-op, was getting £6 a week and they thought themselves not badly off. So it's not the modesty of my mother's aspirations that
5   seems surprising now but the direction. Why gentleman farmers? And the answer, of course, was books.

I had read quite a few story-books by this time, as I had learned to read quite early by dint, it seemed to me, of staring over my brother's shoulder at the comic he was reading until suddenly it made sense. Though I liked reading (and showed off at it), it was soon
10   borne in upon me that the world of books was only distantly related to the world in which I lived. The families I read about were not like our family (no family ever quite was). These families had dogs and gardens and lived in country towns equipped with thatched cottages and mill-streams, where the children had adventures, saved lives, caught villains, and found treasures before coming home, tired but happy, to eat
15   sumptuous teas off chequered tablecloths in low-beamed parlours presided over by comfortable pipe-smoking fathers and gentle aproned mothers, who were invariably referred to as Mummy and Daddy.

In an effort to bring this fabulous world closer to my own, more threadbare, existence, I tried as a first step substituting "Mummy" and "Daddy" for my usual "Mam" and "Dad",
20   but was pretty sharply discouraged. My father was hot on anything smacking of social pretension; there had even been an argument at the font because my aunties had wanted my brother given two Christian names instead of plain one.

Had it been only stories that didn't measure up to the world it wouldn't have been so bad. But it wasn't only fiction that was fiction. Fact too was fiction, as textbooks seemed
25   to bear no more relation to the real world than did the story-books. At school or in my *Boy's Book of the Universe* I read of the minor wonders of nature,—the sticklebacks that haunted the most ordinary pond, the newts and toads said to lurk under every stone, and the dragon-flies that flitted over the dappled surface. Not, so far as I could see, in Leeds. There were owls in hollow trees, so the nature books said, but I saw no owls and hollow
30   trees were in short supply too. It was only in the frog-spawn department that nature actually lined up with the text. Even in Leeds there was that, jamjars of which I duly fetched home to stand beside great wilting bunches of bluebells on the backyard window-sill. But the tadpoles never seemed to graduate to the full-blown frogs the literature predicted, invariably giving up the ghost as soon as they reached the two-legged stage
35   when, unbeknownst to Mam, they would have to be flushed secretly down the lav.

This sense of deprivation, fully developed by the time I was seven or eight, sometimes came down to particular words. I had read in many stories, beginning I suppose with *Babes in the Wood*, how the childish hero and heroine, lost in the forest, had nevertheless spent a cosy night bedded down on *pine needles*. I had never come across these

40 delightfully accommodating features and wondered where they were to be found. Could one come across them in Leeds? It was not short on parks after all—Gott's Park, Roundhay Park—surely one of them would have pine needles.

And then there was *sward*, a word that was always cropping up in *Robin Hood*. It was what tournaments and duels were invariably fought on. But what was sward? "Grass" said

45 my teacher, Miss Timpson, shortly; but I knew it couldn't be. Grass was the wiry, sooty stuff that covered the Ree in Moorfield Road where we played at night after school. That was not sward. So once, hearing of some woods in Bramley, a few miles from where we lived, I went off on the trail of sward, maybe hoping to come across pine needles in the process. I trailed out past the rhubarb fields at Hill Top, over Stanningly Road then down

50 into the valley that runs up from Kirkstall Abbey. But all I found were the same mouldy trees and stringy grass that we had at Armley.

Sticklebacks, owls, hollow trees, pine needles and sward—they were what you read about in books; books which were borrowed from Armley Junior Library, and an institution more intended to discourage children from reading could not have been designed. It was

55 presided over by a fierce British Legion commissionaire, a relic of the Boer War, who with his medals and walrus moustache was the image of Hindenberg as pictured on German stamps in my brother's album.

The few books we actually owned were, in fact, largely reference books, bought by subscription through magazines: *Enquire Within*, *What Everybody Wants to Know* and, with

60 its illustrations of a specimen man and woman (minus private parts), *Everybody's Home Doctor*. Mam, admittedly, sometimes sought her own particular brand of genteel escape— sagas of couples who had thrown up everything to start a small-holding (gentleman-farmers in the making).

My parents always felt that had they been educated, had they been "real readers", their

65 lives and indeed their characters would have been different. They imagined books would make them less shy and (always an ambition) able to "mix". Quiet and never particularly gregarious, they cherished a lifelong longing to "branch out", with books somehow the key to it. This unsatisfied dream they have bequeathed to me, so that without any conscious intention I find I am often including in plays or films a scene where a character

70 shows a desire to enter a prestigious world dominated by books. As for me, while I'm not baffled by books, I can't see how anyone can love them ("He loved books"). I can't see how anyone can "love literature". What does that mean? Of course one advantage to being a gentleman farmer is that you seldom have to grapple with such questions.

Questions on Passage 1

a   Drawing your information from the second paragraph (lines 8–14), give in your own words a reason why it was unusual for the author, as a boy, to be alone in the house.   1   **U**

b   i)   Show how in lines 15–17 the author reinforces the significance of the moment described in the previous paragraphs.

        In your answer you should refer to **one** of the following: sentence structure; imagery; word choice; tense.   2   **A**

     ii)   Choose **one** of the extended images contained in lines 18–23 and show how effective you find it in describing the boy's awakening.   2   **E**

    iii)   "What I saw in fact was pretty banal." (line 24)

        Explain how lines 24–27 ("My father . . . was wonderful.") help you to arrive at the meaning of "banal".   2   **U**

c   i)   By referring to specific words and phrases, explain fully the part lines 39–42 play in the structure of the passage as a whole.   3   **A**

     ii)   Explain how lines 43–44 help you to arrive at the meaning of "the ordinary is just the unique in hiding" (lines 43–45).   2   **U**

d   i)   From lines 46–53, give one feature of the author's home life which ensured that he encountered a wide variety of language.   1   **U**

     ii)   In your own words, explain why the boy was "astonished" (line 58).   1   **U**

    iii)   In lines 54–61, the author uses imagery to convey the special contribution made by his home to his future career.

        By referring to one, or more than one, example, show how effective you find his use of this technique.   2   **A**

e   i)   What is the tone of "If books were not the most sought-after domestic adjuncts in our housing scheme. . ." (lines 71–72)?   1   **A**

     ii)   From the rest of the sentence select a feature of sentence structure **or** word choice which contributes to that tone and explain how it does so.   2   **A**

f   To what extent do you find the anecdote related in lines 80–86 ("It was only . . . in my boyhood") a suitable conclusion to this passage?

     Justify your view by referring to the whole passage.   4   **E**

                                                                                (23)

g   Drawing your information from line 46 to the end of the passage, write a paragraph in which you summarise the main factors which had a positive influence on William McIlvanney's development as a writer.

     Use your own words as far as possible.   (6)   **U**

Questions on Passage 2

h   Give **two** reasons why the writer's mother suggested that he should become a "gentleman-farmer". You should refer to lines 1–6 and lines 60–63 in your answer.   **2   U**

i   i)   Explain briefly in your own words the writer's view about "the world of books" (line 10) and his own life.   **2   U**

    ii)   By referring fully to lines 18–22, explain how the writer develops this view in a humorous way.   **4   U**

j   i)   "Fact too was fiction . . ." (line 24)

       Show how lines 23–25 help you to arrive at the meaning of this statement.   **2   U**

    ii)   By referring to any part of lines 25–35, show briefly how the writer develops in a humorous way his idea that "Fact too was fiction".   **2   U**

k   Look again at lines 36–51 ("This sense of deprivation . . . we had at Armley.")

    Show how effective you find this section of the passage.

    You should refer to ideas and tone in your answer.   **4   E**

l   i)   Explain in your own words the "unsatisfied dream" (line 68) of the writer's parents and the part that books played in it. You should refer to lines 64–68 in your answer.   **2   U**

    ii)   By referring to lines 68–72 ("This unsatisfied . . . does that mean?"), explain how his parents' feelings about books have affected the writer and his work.   **3   U**

                                          (21)

Question on both Passages

m   Which passage do you find more interesting?

    Compare the two passages in terms of their main ideas **and** such stylistic features as point of view, tone, imagery, structure . . .   **(10)   E**

Total (60)

[END OF QUESTION PAPER]

HIGHER   Time: 1 hour 30 minutes   NATIONAL
ENGLISH   QUALIFICATIONS

Paper II: Specimen Question Paper

There are **two parts** to this paper and you should attempt both parts.

Part 1 (Textual Analysis) is worth 30 marks.

In Part 2 (Critical Essay), you should attempt **one** question only, taken from any of the Sections A–D.

Your answer to Part 2 should begin on a fresh page.

Each question in Part 2 is worth 30 marks.

> *Note* You must not use, in Part 2 of this paper, the same text(s) as you have used in your Specialist Study.

Part 1 (Textual Analysis)

You should spend approximately 45 minutes on this part of the paper.

WAITING ROOM

     She waits neatly, bone-china thin,
     in a room tight with memories,
     claustrophobic with possessions,
     rendered down from eighty years,
5   eight Homes and Gardens rooms.

     She waits graciously, bearing
     the graffiti of age. She drizzles
     sherry into fine glasses, tea
     into what is left
10   of wide-brimmed wedding china.

     With the top of her mind
     she is eager to skim off news
     of the family, who married whom
     and when. Names elude her. Tormented,
15   she tries to trap them on her tongue.

     She waits defiantly, fumbling
     to light a cigarette, veins
     snaking across her hands
     like unravelled knitting. A man's face,

20   preoccupied by youth, looks on.

        We leave her, the stick a third leg,
        waiting to obey the gong,
        (Saturday, boiled eggs for tea)
        waiting for the rain to stop,
25   waiting for winter, waiting.

                    Moira Andrew

Analysis   Marks

a   By referring to the language of line 1, state what initial impression of the
    woman is conveyed.   2

b   What do lines 2–10 reveal to you about the woman's past circumstances?

    Show how the language of these lines leads you to make three deductions
    about her past.   6

c   i)   Stanza three (lines 11–15) reveals aspects of the woman's personality.
            Suggest three characteristics of her personality.   3

    ii)   Go on to explain how effectively you think aspects of her personality
            are conveyed. You should refer to such techniques as word choice,
            sentence structure, imagery, sound . . .   3

d   From an examination of the language of lines 16–19 ("She waits defiantly
    . . . like unravelled knitting."), show how sympathy is elicited for the old
    woman.   3

e   "A man's face,
    preoccupied by youth, looks on." (lines 19–20)

    Comment on the significance of these lines in the context of the whole poem.   3

Appreciation

f   Comment on the significance for you of the idea of "waiting" in the whole
    poem. In your answer you should consider the poet's treatment of the idea
    and your reactions to it.   10

Total Marks (30)

[Turn over for PART 2—CRITICAL ESSAY]

Part 2—Critical Essay

Attempt ONE question only, taken from any of the Sections A to D.

In all Sections you may use Scottish texts.

You should spend about 45 minutes on this part of the paper.

Begin your answer on a fresh page.

SECTION A—DRAMA

1 Choose a play in which a character is forced to compromise or refuses to compromise.

   Explain briefly how the situation comes about and go on to discuss how you think the character's decision affects the ideas and the outcome of the play.

   In your answer you must refer closely to the text and to at least two of: key scene(s), theme, climax characterisation or any other appropriate feature.

2 Choose a play whose opening scene seems to you to be particularly amusing or menacing.

   Discuss how effectively the opening scene prepares you for the rest of the play.

   In your answer you must refer closely to the text and to at least two of: exposition, mood, setting, conflict, dialogue, theme or any other appropriate feature.

3 "I am . . . more sinned against than sinning."

   Discuss to what extent you find this an accurate description of a Shakespearean tragic hero or heroine.

   In your answer you must refer closely to the text and to at least two of: theme, characterisation, relationships, soliloquy, key scene(s), conflict or any other appropriate feature.

4. Choose a play in which tension is deliberately created towards the end.

   Explain how the tension is created and go on to discuss how the tension adds to your appreciation of the ending of the play.

   In your answer you must refer closely to the text and to at least two of: conflict, climax, dialogue, structure or any other appropriate feature.

SECTION B—PROSE

5. Choose a novel in which a character's personality appears to change.

   Outline the nature of the change (or the apparent change) and go on to discuss how this illuminates for you the theme(s) of the text.

In your answer you must refer closely to the text and to at least two of: key incident(s), structure, narrative stance, contrast or any other appropriate feature.

6   Choose a novel in which symbolism plays an important part.

Discuss how effectively the symbolism adds to your understanding and appreciation of the characterisation or the ideas in the novel.

In your answer you must refer closely to the text and to at least two of: symbolism, characterisation, theme, setting, structure or any other appropriate feature.

7   Choose a novel or short story in which one character's loyalty or disloyalty to another proves to be decisive.

Explain how this arises and go on to discuss why you think it is important to the text as a whole.

In your answer you must refer closely to the text and to at least two of: key incident(s), characterisation, structure, narrative stance, tone or any other appropriate feature.

8   Choose a novel or a work of non-fiction whose setting contributes significantly to the overall impact of the text.

Discuss the importance of the setting to your understanding and appreciation of the main concerns or issues of the text.

In your answer you must refer closely to the text and to at least two of: setting, theme, style, symbolism or any other appropriate feature.

SECTION C—POETRY

9   Choose a poet whose work has impressed you in terms of both style and content.

Referring to at least two poems, explain what you admire about the poet's work.

In your answer you must refer closely to the text and to at least two of: theme, poetic form, imagery, word-choice or any other appropriate feature.

10 Choose a poem which forces you to face up to an unpleasant truth.

Show how the poet achieves this effect.

In your answer you must refer closely to the text and to at least two of: theme, word-choice, imagery, sound or any other appropriate feature.

11 Choose a poem which you think could be described as a love poem.

Discuss how successfully the poet conveys the emotions in the poem.

In your answer you must refer closely to the text and to at least two of: imagery, symbolism, poetic form, rhyme, rhythm or any other appropriate feature.

12 Choose a dramatic monologue which reveals a particularly admirable or particularly unpleasant character.

Show how the poem leads you to form this opinion.

In your answer you must refer closely to the text and to at least two of: poetic form, tone, setting, sound, word-choice or any other appropriate feature.

SECTION D—MASS MEDIA

13 Choose a film which leads you into the mind of a complex or subtle character.

Explain how the character is created in this film.

In your answer you must refer closely to the text and to at least two of: casting, dialogue, editing, use of camera, clothing, lighting or any other appropriate feature.

14 Choose a film which has something important to say to you about a serious social issue.

Explain how the film conveys the importance of the subject.

In your answer you must refer closely to the text and to at least two of: genre, theme, use of stars, setting, plot, key sequences or any other appropriate feature.

15 Isolation, rejection, confrontation, loneliness are major themes that are explored in many TV dramas.

By referring to one TV drama, discuss how one of these themes is dealt with in a way which you found meaningful.

In your answer you must refer closely to the text and to at least two of: theme, plot, use of camera, lighting, objects, colour, sound track or any other appropriate feature.

16 Many memorable TV dramas leave the viewer with a powerful impression of a person, a place, or an event.

Describe how a TV drama succeeded in creating such an impression for you.

In your answer you must refer closely to the text and to at least two of: genre, casting, colour, music, clothing, dialogue, properties or any other appropriate feature.

[END OF QUESTION PAPER]

CHAPTER TWELVE

REVISION AND STUDY

This final chapter of THE GUIDE is intended to give you some thoughts and ideas about studying and so-called revision. I say 'so-called' because English is hard to revise for in the conventional sense. There are no facts to learn and regurgitate.

As you already know, your study of English is a long development process, an accumulation and reinforcement of skills and knowledge that enable you to use language for reading, writing, talking and listening. It is more to do with 'how', rather than with 'what'.

So, in this context, revision (literally looking back at something, or seeing it again) means considering what you have already experienced in the course. That will involve revisiting your work on all four modes of language.

Since English involves *developing* skills, you can't learn about it at the last minute before the exam. The best approach is to do the work (i.e. the learning) at the time of teaching, and to make sure by asking and discussing that you understand at that time.

However, there's no denying that revisiting your work near the exam time (when you are required to express your ideas, skills and knowledge) is a sensible idea. Spending long hours at this right before the exams is, though, counter-productive. You should do your revision in short and reasonable stints over a longer period. Studying for long, lonely hours is not the best way.

The evening and night before an exam is definitely not the time to be studying, regardless of what your panicky friends are doing. Spend that time relaxing and be confident for the next day.

The chapter ends with some final notes on study and revision for English.

Think about time-management and plan your work:

- Don't sacrifice your sleeping time.
- Work for short fixed periods of time.
- Work to a fixed routine.
- Make a timetable or schedule for all your subjects.
- Balance reading and timed writing tasks.

Think of useful aids to your working time:

- Operate a buddy-system with a friend.
- Play music if that helps . . . but music without lyrics.
- Take regular breaks and go out for fresh air.
- Have coffee, tea or coke breaks.

Be systematic in your learning:

- Ask for help *at the time* that you don't understand.
- Make notes and use them right away, not months later.
- Start studying/revising long before your exams.
- Don't memorise notes: learn what they *mean*.
- Really listen in class.
- Spend time daily on improving spelling, punctuation and vocabulary. Reading is a good way to learn.

Make use of resources for learning:

- Re-read your literary texts.
- Use past exam papers.
- Use your notes.
- Consult websites.
- Read newspapers of quality.
- Practise answering questions and become familiar with question formats.

This is the end of THE GUIDE. Don't forget to use the Index and the Glossary. I wish you the best of success in your Higher English.

GLOSSARY

an	indefinite article used always before initial vowel (and before silent consonants)
appeal	request (by your school/college only) to SQA to re-examine your exam performance
belies	gives a false or unexpected notion of something
broadsheet	large format newspaper
complacency	self-satisfaction, lack of concern
comprise(s)	consist(s) of
concepts	ideas
context	text surrounding expression in question
continuous	repeated from time to time, not continual
déjà vu	having been seen already
doric	alternative form of any language (originally Doric, from Doria, i.e. not from Athens)
epitaph	(here) the words on a gravestone, the last words
exhaustive	comprehensive, including everything
ferm loun	a young male farm-worker
folio	a folder to contain papers
genre	a type or category of writing
hackneyed	worn out, over-used (as in hackney carriage, one use for hiring out)
hierarchy	order of importance
holistic	undivided, whole, uncompartmented
homophone	word having the same sound (pronunciation) as another
hyperbole	deliberate exaggeration for effect
invaluable	so important that it cannot have a value set upon it; priceless
irony	figure of speech using bitter humour, sarcasm, and expressed as the opposite
jargon	words of expressions used by a particular group or profession
mode	form or type, means
monologue	words spoken by a single person uninterrupted
nominally	in name only, not in practice
OHT	overhead transparency
paradox	statement which appears at first to be self-contradictory
pejorative	tending to reduce in value
phenomenon	a natural wonder (plural, phenomena)
polarise	set at opposite points
regurgitate	bring back up what has been swallowed
relationship	connection, in widest sense, ie, not only sexual
rhetorical	(as in question) – assuming a preferred answer

rubric	detailed instruction (originally the (highlighted) red-printed sections of missal/bible)
semantic	the meaning attached to words
spectrum	a range (originally of colours, as in a rainbow)
syntax	the rules of grammar
tabloid	a small-sized format of newspaper, usually sensational

INDEX